new BIRTH TO FIVE

A complete guide to the first five years
of being a parent

Contents

About this book

No one needs a book to tell them what's good about being a parent. Parents turn to books when they need information, when they're worried, when they've got questions or worries, small or large. This is a book you can turn to.

1 The first weeks

There's something very special, and exciting, about being alone for the first time with your new baby, but it can also be frightening. This is when you begin to realise that you can never go back. You're now responsible for a new human being. The responsibility may seem much too big. You may have a secret wish to run home to your own mother and ask her to take over. Or you may be the kind of person who just knows that you'll get through and that everything will turn out fine in the end.

In these early weeks you'll find there's a great deal to learn, and all of it at the same time. Think of these first few pages as a guide to the basic information you'll need to survive. Today it might seem impossible. In a matter of months you'll look back and wonder how it could've all seemed so hard. Read Chapter 7 for more on how having a baby changes your life.

HOW YOU FEEL

COPING WITH THE FIRST FEW WEEKS

- Make your baby your first task and try not to worry about everything else.
- Ask for help from your partner, mother, or friends. Sometimes people with small babies of their own can be the most help because they know what it's like.

"I don't think I'll ever forget those first few days. Feeling so happy, though I don't know why. I couldn't sleep, I was sore, I couldn't move about very well, but I felt happier than I can ever begin to say."

"There was none of this love at first sight. It was a long time before I came to love him. I can say that now, but at the time I couldn't tell anybody. I thought there was something wrong with me. There was all that work, and feeling rough myself, and because I didn't have this overwhelming feeling for him, none of it made much sense. But oh yes, after three or four months or so of all that, yes, it came right then."

(A father) "I didn't think I'd feel the way I do about her. Sometimes I look at her when she's sleeping, you know, and I have to put my face down next to hers, just to check she's breathing."

- Accept help and suggest to people what they can do: cook a meal and bring it round; do a stack of washing up; do bits of shopping when you run out.
- Sleep whenever your baby allows you to.
- Practise relaxation techniques (see page 112).
- Keep a good supply of nutritious snacks, like fruit, milk, and wholemeal bread, which you can eat without cooking.
- See friends when *you* want to, and if you're tired, tell your friends and suggest that they leave and come back later.
- Remember, this period is hard but it lasts for a relatively short time and it does get better.

Emergencies
In these early days when you're just getting to know your baby, you may not be able to tell what is simply a change from normal and what is a real problem. Never be afraid to ask. Your GP, health visitor, and midwife are there to help you while you learn about your own baby's behaviour. Never feel ashamed of asking for help and advice if you're worried whatever time it is, day or night. See page 79–80 for how to know when your baby is ill.

FEELING BLUE (POSTNATAL DEPRESSION)

In the first few days you may be weepy and irritable. Your mood may swing up and down from dizzy happiness to total despair. Usually your feelings start to even out after a few days, though you may find that tiredness makes you feel very touchy and sensitive.

Sometimes the despair doesn't lift. If you find that you can't sleep even when you've the chance, that you're not eating well, and that nothing seems to shift you out of your misery, you need to ask for help.

Postnatal depression is a very real problem for some new mothers. You or your partner or friends can talk to your GP or health visitor or contact the Association for Post Natal Illness or a support organisation such as MAMA (see page 133). Sometimes it's enough just to find someone to talk to. For more serious depression your doctor may be able to help. There's more about how you may feel on page 113.

BREASTFEEDING

If you've decided to breastfeed your baby, you already know that it's the best thing to do. If your baby's born prematurely then breastfeeding is even more beneficial. You may find you've no problems at all and that apart from perhaps a bit of nipple tenderness at the start, it's a real comfort and a pleasure. On the other hand quite a lot of first-time mothers find the early weeks of breastfeeding hard. Keep going, get help if you need it, and have confidence. If you learn how to do it and sort out any problems, breastfeeding will be as good for you as it is for your baby, as well as being convenient and cheap.

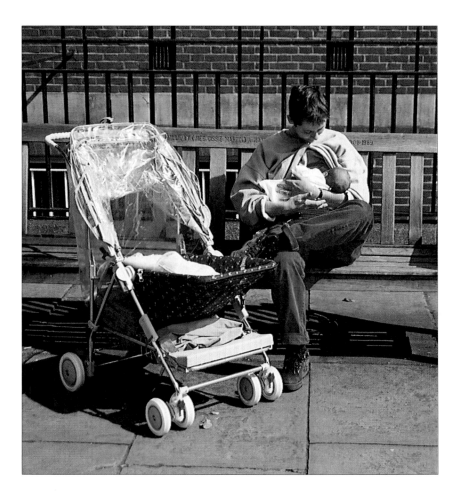

HOW BREASTFEEDING WORKS

Understanding how breastfeeding works can help you make it work.

Your milk supply

Your breasts produce milk in response to your baby feeding at your breast. The more your baby feeds, the more milk you produce. So, if you let your baby feed whenever he or she wants a feed, you're likely to produce the amount of milk your baby needs. Feeding more often will increase your milk supply.

The 'let-down' reflex

Your baby's feeding causes the 'let-down' of your milk. It makes your milk flow down and gather behind your nipple. Sometimes this happens even before your baby starts to feed, maybe when you hear your baby cry. In the early weeks, milk may start to leak from your breasts.

The let-down reflex is important. Without it, your baby can't get your milk easily. For the reflex to work, you need to be fairly relaxed. Stress, worry, exhaustion, pain, even embarrassment can all stop the let-down reflex working. If you're anxious and under stress, it may not seem to be very helpful to be told to stop worrying and relax. But it's probably what you need to do, if you can only find a way of doing it. And if you've any worry or problem over feeding, ask for help (see box on page 10).

How your baby feeds

Unlike the teat on a bottle, there's no milk in the nipple itself. The breasts are never empty, but the milk has to be let down so that it can gather behind the nipple and areola (the dark area around the nipple). A baby who only sucks on the nipple doesn't get much milk (and may hurt your nipples). To make the milk flow out, your baby has to be in the right position at your breast (see page 8). Make sure your baby's mouth is wide open and that your baby's gums press against the area around the nipple. It's your baby's tongue that will do most of the work, pressing the milk out from the milk glands underneath the nipple. The pictures on this page and page 8 will give you a clearer idea.

FINDING THE RIGHT POSITION

For you

Make yourself comfortable. You'll need to hold your baby close to your breast without strain and for some time, so do make sure that your back is well supported all the way down. Try different chairs and different ways of sitting, and perhaps a footstool to raise your legs. Try lying down on your side with your baby up against you. Find what's best for you.

Later, you won't have to think about what position you're in. You'll be able to feed almost however and wherever you want to.

The advantages of breastfeeding
● Breast milk is the only food **naturally** designed and meant for your baby. It contains the nutrients your baby needs for health and development. Breast milk is easily digested. It's less likely to cause stomach upsets or diarrhoea. It helps avoid constipation.
● Breast milk also contains antibodies and other protective factors, which help your baby fight against infections. Formula milk used for bottle feeding doesn't help fight infections. So breastfed babies are less likely to fall ill or be admitted to hospital.
● Breastfed babies are less likely to get allergies like eczema.
● Research shows that premature babies who have received breast milk may have better long-term development.
● Breastfeeding is practical. There's no cost or preparation, and the milk's always available at the right temperature – even in the middle of the night!

For your baby

Bring your baby up to your breast rather than trying to bring your breast to your baby. Try using a pillow to raise your baby higher.

Hold your baby close and turned towards you. Your baby's chest and not his or her side should be against you. Make sure your baby's mouth is in line with your nipple. You can make your baby turn towards your breast by gently rubbing your nipple against your baby's cheek.

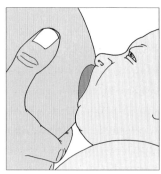

Your baby needs to take in your nipple and much of the area around your nipple (more below than above) with a wide-open mouth.

As your baby fixes on, make sure his or her chin is against your breast and that your baby's lower lip is turned out. The lower jaw does the work of feeding.

If it doesn't feel right, slide one of your fingers into your baby's mouth to gently break the suction. Then, as your baby's mouth opens wide in protest, try fixing your baby on again. Keep trying until it feels right and you can see your baby taking big long swallows. Your baby may stop and start or feed quite steadily.

HOW OFTEN, HOW LONG?

Some babies settle into a pattern of feeding quite quickly. Others take longer. In the early weeks, you may find that your baby's feeds are sometimes long, sometimes short, sometimes close together, sometimes further apart. Try to follow what your baby tells you. Feed when your baby asks to be fed, and for as long as your baby wants.

Once you've put your baby to your breast, let the feed go on until your baby wants to stop. Then, either straight away or after a pause, offer the other breast to see if your baby wants more. If you swap from one breast to the other before your baby is ready, you may only be giving your baby the thinner 'foremilk' from each breast. The 'hindmilk' which comes later is richer and contains calories that your baby needs.

Allow your baby to decide when he or she has had enough. Both breasts won't always be wanted at each feed. Your baby will show that he or she has finished by either letting go of your breast or falling asleep. Start each feed on alternate breasts or you may get painfully engorged (see page 10). You could remind yourself by tying a ribbon, or pinning a safety pin, to the bra strap on the side you last used.

If you feed as often and for as long as your baby wants, you'll produce plenty of milk and give your baby what he or she needs. While your baby is very young, this may mean quite lengthy feeds. But if you've got your baby in the right position at your breast, you shouldn't become sore.

At first it may seem that you're doing nothing but feeding. Remember that this stage will not last very long. If you can relax, and let go of most other things in these early weeks you'll find that your milk supply increases and so will the speed with which your baby feeds. Babies have growth spurts and may feed more frequently at these times until your milk supply increases to meet the bigger demand.

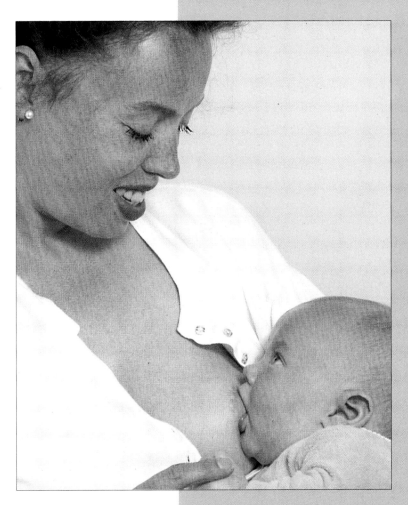

HOW MUCH IS ENOUGH?

Since it's impossible to see how much milk your baby is taking from your breast, you may wonder whether your baby is getting enough. You can be sure you're giving enough milk if your baby:

- has at least six really wet nappies a day and is having nothing but breast milk;
- is generally gaining weight. It is overall weight gain that's important: some babies gain weight steadily, other perfectly healthy babies gain little or no weight one week, then feed more often and make up for it over the next week or two (see pages 34–5).

If, at any time during the first two to three months, your baby is feeding less than five to six times in 24 hours or is gaining weight only slowly, talk to your midwife or health visitor.

Night feeds are especially high in nutrients. When your baby is small it's important for these to continue.

If your baby seems unusually sleepy and is slow to start feeding, he or she may be ill, so contact your GP.

HUNGER, OR THIRST?

Breast milk is drink and food in one. If the weather is hot, your baby may want to feed more often. There's no need to give your baby drinks of water even in a very hot climate.

BREASTFEEDING PROBLEMS

"My nipples hurt when she feeds. What can I do?"
During the first week or two, many breastfeeding mothers feel some discomfort as their baby starts sucking. Your milk supply has to settle down, and your nipples have to grow used to your baby's sucking. After this, if feeding still hurts, your baby's position is wrong. If you can't get the position right yourself, ask for help.

"I've been feeding my baby for two weeks now, but my nipple is cracked and painful. Should I give up?"
If your baby is in the right position at your breast, feeding shouldn't hurt.

- Check that your baby is fixing properly. Ask for help if you need it. Once your baby is positioned correctly cracks should heal rapidly.
- Keep your nipples clean and dry, but avoid soap which dries the skin too much.
- Change breast pads frequently. Avoid pads with plastic backing.
- Wear a cotton bra and let the air get to your nipples as much as possible.
- Try sleeping topless with a towel under you if you're leaking milk.
- A few drops of milk rubbed into the nipple at the end of a feed may help.
- Thrush in your baby's mouth can sometimes cause sore nipples. Thrush is an infection that results in small white patches, which don't wipe away. If you think your baby has thrush, both you and your baby will need medical treatment, so see your GP.
- If your nipples remain sore ask a health visitor for advice.

"He stops and starts and cries and just doesn't seem to settle down."
If your baby is restless at your breast and doesn't seem satisfied by feeds, he or she may be sucking on the nipple alone and not getting enough milk. Check your baby is in the right position and fixed properly to your breast. Ask for help if you need to.

"My breasts are very swollen and hard and painful. What's wrong?"
You're 'engorged' (full of milk). This is common in the first few weeks or if your baby has gone a long time between feeds. The answer is to feed your baby. If feeding is difficult for some reason, ask for help. To ease the swelling, try a hot bath or bathe your breasts with warm water. Smooth out some milk with your fingers, stroking gently downwards towards the nipple. Or try holding a face cloth wrung out in very cold water against your breast. Check your bra's not too tight.

"I have a hard, painful lump in my breast. What is it?"
It's probably a blocked milk duct. Milk builds up because the ducts aren't being emptied properly. Check that your bra isn't too tight and that nothing is pressing into your breast as you feed (your bra or arm, for example).

A good feed on the blocked breast will help. As you feed, smooth the milk away from the blockage towards the nipple. If this doesn't work, ask for help. If left untreated, blocked ducts can lead to mastitis (see below).

"There is a red, hot, painful patch on my breast and I feel quite unwell. Why?"
You may have mastitis. Don't stop feeding as you need to keep your milk moving. Try different positions to empty different parts of your breast. Try the suggestions for relieving engorged breasts and blocked ducts and get lots of rest. Go to bed if you can and contact your doctor. You may well need antibiotics to clear the infection. Your doctor can prescribe one that is safe to take while breastfeeding.

Help with breastfeeding
You can get help and advice from:
- your community midwife, health visitor, or GP;
- a breastfeeding counsellor or support group. Contact your local branch of the National Childbirth Trust or La Leche League (see pages 133–6). These organisations can provide you with help and support from other mothers with experience of breastfeeding.

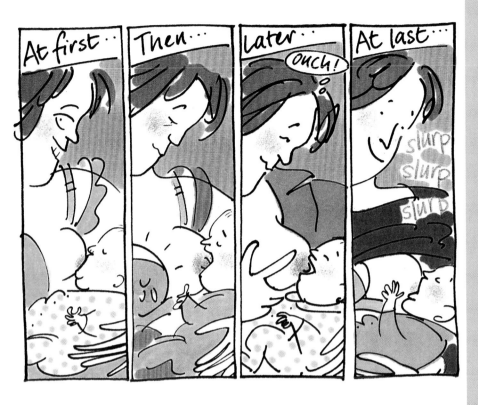

MAKING BREASTFEEDING WORK FOR YOU

Breastfeeding will work best if you're enjoying it as much as your baby. Try to find ways of making it fit in with the way you feel about things.

Some mothers are happy to feed anywhere and in front of anyone. You may prefer to wear a top that you can pull upwards so that you can feed discreetly, rather than one that unbuttons, which may leave you feeling exposed.

Other mothers find breastfeeding in front of others awkward and embarrassing. You may feel that it's just easier to live a very private life for the first few months with your baby. That's fine. Don't feel under pressure to socialise if you don't want to. When you do go out, ask if there is another room where you can feed your baby. Many shops and public places now provide mothers' rooms. Do what feels best for you.

EXPRESSING MILK

If you want to express milk in the first few weeks (perhaps because your baby is in Special Care), ask your midwife about it. Hospitals often keep machines for people who need to express milk and you can be shown how to use it. Alternatively you may be told how to hire one.

Unless there's a special reason for expressing milk, it's usually easier not to try it until you've got breastfeeding well established. After six weeks or so you may want to express milk for someone else to give to your baby in a bottle.

If you've plenty of milk you'll probably find expressing quite easy, particularly if you do it in the morning. Some mothers however find it quite difficult. Your midwife or health visitor will show you how to express milk using a pump or by hand.

You must express your milk into a sterilised bottle, which you can then cap and store in the fridge. Don't keep it for longer than 24 hours. You can also freeze breast milk if you want to keep it for a few weeks. When you want to use it, put it in the fridge until completely defrosted but then treat it as you would bottled milk (see pages 14–15).

COMBINING BREAST AND BOTTLE
In the early weeks

If you think you're not producing enough milk for your baby you may want to give your baby an occasional bottle. But, if you really do want to breastfeed, it is best to stick with it, at least for the first six weeks. Otherwise, as your baby feeds less from you, you will produce less milk and you may end up weaning your baby off your breast completely. Of course, this may be the right solution if breastfeeding is making you unhappy.

If you've started giving the odd bottle, but then decide you want to go back to full breastfeeding, you can, but you will have to breastfeed your baby often and for longer to increase your milk supply. For a day or two your baby may cry more and feed more, but this won't go on for long. Feeds will space out again once your milk supply has increased.

Once breastfeeding is well established

You've more flexibility for combining breast and bottle at this later stage. You can introduce a regular bottle feed of formula milk if, for example, you're returning to work, or simply want someone else involved in feeding. If you offer the bottle feed at the same time each day your own supply will adjust quite quickly and you should be able to keep on breastfeeding at the other feeds. Mothers returning to work, for example, often breastfeed in the morning and evening and their babies have a cup or bottle of formula during the day.

CHANGING FROM BREAST TO BOTTLE

If you're having difficulty breastfeeding, and decide to change to bottle feeding, you're unlikely to experience difficulty getting your baby to take a bottle and you'll probably both feel more relaxed when feeding settles down.
The problems arise when your baby enjoys breastfeeding, and you need to get him or her to take a bottle, perhaps because you're returning to work, or for some other reason.

> Remember that your baby will gain a unique advantage from breast milk if you breastfeed exclusively for three months. This gives your baby the best start to life.

You may find it easier to change over to infant formula using a cup. There is no reason why you *have* to use a bottle.

Give yourself time for the changeover and start well before your return to work. It's probably best not to give the first bottle feed at times when your baby is tired and it may help if someone other than you gives the first feeds. Your baby is not then near your breast, smelling and expecting breast milk. Don't panic if you experience difficulties at first. Your baby will get used to the new arrangements in time.

BOTTLE FEEDING

Get well organised for bottle feeding so that you can enjoy it. In time, you'll find your own routine for preparing feeds and sterilising.

WHAT YOU'LL NEED

- **At least six bottles and teats** There are different kinds of bottles and teats. Ask your midwife, health visitor, or other mothers if you want advice on what to buy. You may be offered second-hand bottles. Make sure they're not scratched – if they are, you won't be able to sterilise them properly. Always buy new teats.
- **A supply of baby milk (formula milk)** There are lots of different brands of baby milk and you may want advice on which to choose. Most formula milks are made from cow's milk that has been specially treated to make it suitable for babies. If there's a strong history of allergies in your family and you can't breastfeed, seek advice as early as possible from your GP or health visitor. You may be referred to a paediatrician or immunologist (a doctor with a special interest in allergies). Don't experiment with non-dairy milks with a newborn baby because they can also trigger allergies. Milk is usually sold cheaply in clinics but can be cheaper still in large supermarkets so it's worth comparing prices (see 'Help with national health service costs' page 131, to check whether you can claim free or low-price milk for your baby).
- **Sterilising equipment** See page 14.

Bottle feeding help and advice
If you want help or advice on bottle feeding, talk to your midwife or health visitor, or to other mothers with experience of bottle feeding.

Making up feeds

● **To make up milk, always put the water in first and then follow the instructions on the tin or packet exactly.**

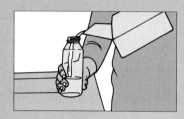

Don't add extra powder or anything else, like baby rice, to make a 'stronger' feed as your baby may not be able to digest it properly. In some cases this could even make him or her ill.

● **You can make up a day's feeds in advance and store the capped bottles in the fridge. This saves time, and means you don't have to make your baby wait while you make up a feed – although you will need six or seven bottles and teats. Don't keep the made-up milk for longer than 24 hours and shake the bottle well before you use it.**

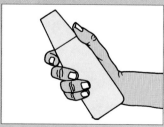

● **If your baby doesn't finish a bottle, don't keep the extra. Throw it away.**

WASHING AND STERILISING

Your bottles and teats must be washed and sterilised to protect your baby against infection.

Washing

Wash your baby's bottles and teats thoroughly using washing-up liquid. If you've been advised to use salt to clean the teats, use as little as possible and rinse it off thoroughly. Get rid of every trace of milk, squirting water through the teats and using a bottle brush for the bottles.

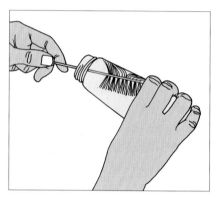

Rinse in clean water.

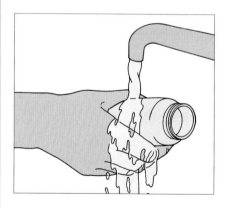

Sterilising

There are a number of different ways of sterilising.

Chemical sterilising

You can buy a complete sterilising unit in the shops or use a plastic bucket with a lid.

● To make up the solution, follow the instructions that come with the sterilising tablets or liquid.

● Immerse your baby's washed bottles, lids, and teats in sterilising solution. Leave them in the solution for the time given in the instructions. If you're using a bucket, keep everything under the water by putting a plate on top. Make sure there aren't any air bubbles inside the bottles and don't add any other unsterilised things to the container later or you will have to start all over again.

● When you take the bottles and teats out to make up your baby's feeds, wash your own hands first. Don't rinse the bottles and teats with tap water because you'll make them unsterile again. If you want to rinse off the sterilising solution, use boiled, cooled water.

Sterilising by boiling

● Put washed equipment into a large pan with a lid. Make sure no air is trapped in the bottles.

● Boil for at least ten minutes. Leave everything in the covered pan until needed.

● Keep the pan out of the reach of older children.

● Keep your pan only for bottles.

● Teats that are boiled regularly get sticky and need replacing regularly.

Steam sterilisers

There are steam sterilisers specially designed for bottles which are both quick and efficient.

Microwave bottle sterilisers

These are designed specifically for sterilising bottles. Never use an ordinary microwave to sterilise bottles.

FEEDING

- You can warm your baby's bottle before a feed by standing it in some hot water. Test the temperature of the milk by squirting some on to your wrist. Some babies don't mind cold milk, others like it warmed. Don't give a baby milk that has been kept warm for more than an hour before a feed: germs breed in the warmth. It's dangerous to use a microwave oven to warm a bottle of milk. The milk continues to heat for a time after you take it out of the microwave, although the outside of the bottle may feel cold.
- Get yourself comfortable so that you can cuddle your baby close as you feed. Give your baby time, and let him or her take as much milk as he or she wants. Some babies take some milk and drop off to sleep, then wake up for more. Be patient. At the end of a feed, throw away any leftover milk.
- As you feed, keep the bottle tilted so that the teat is always full of milk. Otherwise your baby will be taking in air.
- If the teat flattens while you're feeding, pull gently on the bottle to release the vacuum. If the teat blocks, start again with another sterile teat.
- Teats come in all sorts of shapes and with different hole sizes. You may need to experiment to find the right teat and hole size for your baby. If the hole's too small, your baby will suck and suck without getting enough milk. If it's too big, your baby will get too much too quickly and probably spit and splutter or bring the feed back. A small teat hole can be made larger with a red-hot needle if the teat is made of latex. If it is made of silicone you shouldn't try to enlarge the hole, it makes it more likely to tear, and bits could break off into your baby's mouth.
- Never prop up a bottle and leave your baby to feed alone: he or she may choke.
- Don't add solids to bottle feeds. Your baby can't digest them and may choke.

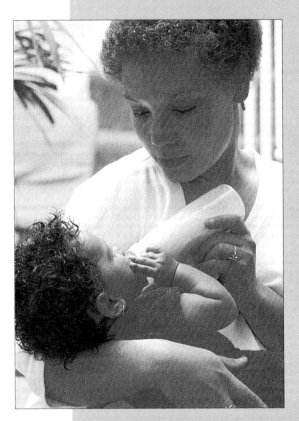

Thirst
If you think your baby is more thirsty than hungry, perhaps because the weather is hot, try a bottle of tap water that has been boiled first and then cooled. Don't use bottled mineral water – it may contain salts unsuitable for a baby.

WIND – AND WHAT MAY COME WITH IT

If your baby swallows a lot of air while feeding and is then put down to sleep, the trapped wind may cause discomfort and your baby may cry. After a feed, it may help to hold your baby upright against your shoulder or propped forward on your lap. Then gently rub your baby's back so that any trapped air can find its way up and out quite easily. Some babies are never troubled by wind, others seem to suffer discomfort after every feed. For information about colic, see page 20.

Some babies sick up more than others. (Sicking up milk during or just after a feed is called 'possetting'.)

15

It's not unusual for a baby to sick up quite a bit. Have a cloth handy to mop up. If your baby brings back a lot of milk, remember he or she is likely to be hungry again quite quickly. If this happens often or if your baby is frequently or violently sick, or if you're worried for any other reason, see your health visitor or GP.

SLEEPING

Some babies sleep much more than others. Some sleep in long patches, some in short. Some soon sleep right through the night, some not for a long time. Your baby will have his or her own pattern of waking and sleeping, and it's unlikely to be the same as other babies you know. Also, the pattern will change over time.

One thing is certain. In the early weeks your baby's sleeping pattern is very unlikely to fit in with your need for sleep. Try to follow your baby's needs. You'll gradually get to know when sleep is needed. Don't catch up on housework while your baby sleeps. Snatch sleep and rest whenever you can.

A baby who wants to sleep isn't likely to be disturbed by household noise. So there's no need to keep the house silent while your baby sleeps. In fact it will help you if your child gets used to sleeping through a certain amount of noise.

Most parents want their children to learn to sleep for the longest period at night – when they are sleeping – and it helps if you encourage night-time sleeping right from the start by teaching your baby that the night-time is different from daytime. During night feeds:

- keep the lights down low
- keep your voice low and don't talk much
- put your baby down as soon as you have fed and changed him or her
- don't change your baby if a change is not needed.

If your baby always falls asleep in your or your partner's arms, at your breast, or with someone by the cot, he or she may not easily take to settling alone. This may not matter to you. But if you want your baby to get used to going off to sleep alone it's wise to start right from the beginning, by putting him or her down before he or she falls asleep.

Once you've established a pattern you may want to try and shift things around a bit. For example, you may wake your baby for a feed just before you go to bed in the hope that you'll get a good long stretch before he or she wakes again.

See pages 55–6 for more information about sleeping problems in older babies and children. Cry-sis, the organisation for parents of crying babies, can also offer help with sleeping problems (address on page 133).

"It wasn't that she wouldn't sleep when she needed to. She just didn't need it. Or at least, she needed a whole lot less than we did. It's not getting your baby to sleep that's the problem; it's getting enough sleep yourself."

"I would just get one of them off to sleep when the other one woke for a feed. I was desperately tired but gradually they got into a pattern and at last I could get some sleep myself."

Disturbed nights can be very hard to bear. If you're bottle feeding, encourage your partner to share the feeds. Many fathers find this a valuable time for getting to know their babies. If you're breastfeeding, your partner may be happy to take over the early morning changing and dressing so that you can go back to sleep. If you're on your own, you could ask a friend or relative to stay for a few days so that you can sleep.

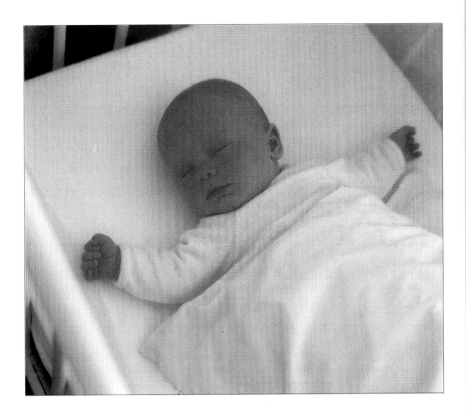

SAFE SLEEPING

Reducing the risk of cot death

Sadly we don't know why some babies die suddenly and for no apparent reason from what is called cot death or Sudden Infant Death Syndrome (SIDS). This section lists in detail all the advice we now have for reducing the risk of cot death and other dangers such as suffocation. There are three ways in which parents can reduce the risk.

- **Always put your baby to sleep on his or her back.**
- **Avoid dressing your baby too warmly or overheating the room (see below).**
- **Don't smoke or allow others to smoke near your baby.**

A safe place to sleep

- Your baby should always be put to sleep on his or her back unless there's clear medical advice to do something different. Babies sleeping on their backs *aren't* more likely to choke and the risk of cot death is increased for babies sleeping on their fronts.
- Avoid ties on plastic sheets or bumpers, ribbons, and bits of string from mobiles. If they're anywhere near your baby, he or she could get tangled in them.
- Make sure there's no gap between the cot mattress and the sides of the cot through which your baby's body could slip. (This is particularly important if you replace the mattress with a new or secondhand one.)
- Remove any loose plastic covering from the mattress that could come off and smother your baby.

Don't leave your baby alone with a bottle as a way of getting him or her off to sleep. There's a danger of choking.

The right temperature

Small babies aren't very good at controlling their own temperature. It's just as important to avoid getting too hot as it is to avoid getting chilled. Overheating is known to be a factor in cot death.

- **If the room is warm enough for you to be comfortable wearing light clothing (16°–20° C) then it's the right temperature for your baby.**
- **Give your baby one light layer of clothing (or bedding) more than you're wearing.** If the room is hot for you, keep your baby's clothes or bed covering light.
- **Don't use duvets (quilts) until your baby is a year old.** They get too hot.
- **Keep your baby's head uncovered** (unless it's very cold) because he or she needs to lose heat from his or her head and face.
- **Never use a hot water bottle or electric blanket.** Babies have delicate skin, which can scald easily.
- **Ill or feverish babies don't need any extra bedding.** In fact they usually need less.
- There's been some advice suggesting that it's unwise to have your baby in bed with you. There's no clear evidence of risk, but it would be wise not to have your baby in your bed if you've been drinking alcohol and to be careful not to let your baby get too hot.
- Babies chill easily if it's cold so **wrap them up well when you go out, but remember to take off the extra clothing when you come back inside** – even if you have to wake your baby to do it.

Clean air

Babies shouldn't be exposed to tobacco smoke, either before birth or afterwards. If you, or anyone else who looks after your baby, smokes, then don't smoke anywhere near the baby. It would be even better if everyone could make an effort to give up completely. Babies and young children who breathe in cigarette smoke are also more likely to get coughs, asthma attacks, and chest and ear infections. For more on smoking see page 110.

CRYING

A lot of people seem to think that babies shouldn't cry. They think that if babies do cry, there must be a reason and you, the parent, should be able to do something about it. But all babies cry, and some cry a lot. Sometimes you'll know the reason. Often you'll try everything to stop it: change nappies, feed, rock, play, and yet nothing seems to work.

If your baby seems at all unwell, seek medical advice early and quickly. Do remember that cot death is rare. Don't let worrying about cot death spoil the first precious months you have with your baby.

Here are some things you can try.

- **Let your baby suckle at your breast.**
- **Hold your baby close**, rocking, swaying, talking, singing. Or put your baby in a sling, held close against you. Move gently about, sway, dance.
- **Rock your baby** backwards and forwards in the pram, or go out for a walk or a drive. Quite a lot of babies sleep in cars and even if your baby wakes up again the minute you stop, you've at least had a break.
- **Find things to look at or listen to:** music on the radio or tape, a rattle, a mobile above the cot.
- **If your baby is bottle fed you can give him or her a dummy**, sterilised for small babies, never sweetened. Some babies find their thumb instead. Later, some will use a bit of cloth as a comforter; you can wash this as often as you need.
- **Stroke your baby firmly and rhythmically** holding him or her against you or lying face downwards on your lap. Or undress your baby and massage with baby oil, gently and firmly. Talk soothingly as you do it. Make sure the room is warm enough.
- **Give your baby a warm bath.** This calms some babies instantly, but makes others cry even more. Like everything else, it might be worth a try.
- **Quietly put your baby down after a feed and leave the room for a few minutes.** Sometimes all the rocking and singing succeeds only in keeping your baby awake.

"At first it really upset me. I felt I ought to be able to comfort him, I ought to be able to make him happy, and he wasn't happy, and I couldn't comfort him, no matter what I did. And then it went on so long, it felt like forever, and I was still upset but I got sort of worn out by it, almost angry, because I was so disappointed that things weren't like I wanted them to be. I wanted to enjoy him, and I wanted him to be like other babies, smiling, gurgling, all of that, and he was just dreadful with the crying."

"It was every evening. We'd be there, rocking her and walking up and down. We got so exhausted we were desperate. And then it stopped, gradually. You don't think you can bear it, but you do bear it, because there's nothing else for it. And in the end, it stops."

(A father) "At some points I just didn't want to be involved at all. The first few months it was so much of a shock... I think that first bit – the sleepless broken nights and constant crying – I just couldn't handle it. I could quite easily have left it all to her, but then gradually I got used to it and you start to bond with the baby."

Remember that this difficult time won't last forever. Your baby will gradually start to take more interest in the things around him or her and the miserable, frustrated crying will almost certainly stop. But if you're finding it hard to cope you may need some help or support. Look on pages 112–14 for suggestions.

COLIC

Many babies have particular times in the day when they cry and cry, and are difficult to comfort. The early evening is the usual bad patch. This is hard on you since it's probably the time when you are most tired and least able to cope.

Crying like this can be due to colic. Everybody agrees that colic exists, but there's disagreement about what causes it or even if there is always a cause. Some doctors say that it's a kind of stomach cramp, and it does seem to cause the kind of crying that might go with waves of stomach pain – very miserable and distressed, stopping for a moment or two, then starting up again. The crying can go on for some hours, and there may be little you can do except try to comfort your baby, and wait for the crying to pass.

- **Try holding your baby in a way that puts gentle pressure and warmth on his or her stomach.** Try face down across your lap, or against your shoulder. Rhythmically rub and stroke your baby's back.
- **If you bottle feed your baby**, talk to your doctor or health visitor about it. They may suggest switching to a different formula milk, but only do this if your doctor or health visitor advises it.
- **If you're breastfeeding**, it may be that something in your diet is upsetting your baby. When your baby seems colicky and uncomfortable, it may be worth looking back over what you've eaten in the last 24 hours. Make a note and discuss it with your health visitor. She may advise cutting out some foods for a while.

Coping with a colicky baby is extremely stressful. It may be best to tell yourself that there's nothing very much you can do. You just need to hang on as best you can until this part of your baby's life is over, which will certainly be in a few weeks. Just knowing that you're not causing the crying and you can't do much to prevent it, may make it easier for you to bear. Try to take some time out for yourself whenever you can. Maybe just handing over to someone else so that you can have a long, hot soak in the bath in the evening. Make sure that you get a decent meal every day to keep up your energy. If a crying baby occupies all your evening, then make lunch your main meal.

IF THE STRAIN GETS TOO MUCH

There may well be times when you're so tired, you feel desperate, angry, and feel you can't take any more. Don't be ashamed to ask for help.

- **Try to share the crying times.** Think about handing your baby over to someone else for an hour. Nobody can cope alone with a constantly crying baby. You need someone who'll give you a break, at least occasionally, to calm down and get some rest.
- **Think about putting your baby down in the cot or pram and going away for a while.** Make sure your baby is safe, close the door, go into another room, and do what you can to calm yourself down. Set a time limit – say, ten minutes – then go back.
- **Ask your health visitor if she knows of any local support for parents of crying babies.** Some areas run a telephone helpline. An organisation called Cry-sis has branches in many areas and offers support through mothers who have had crying babies themselves. See page 133 for details of this and other support organisations.

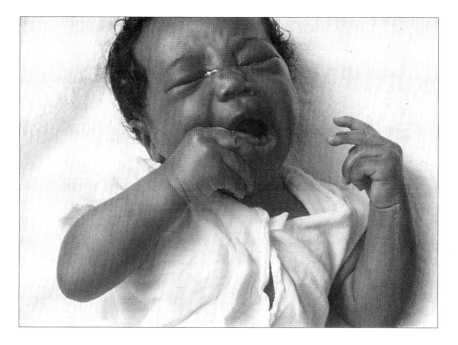

NAPPIES

WHAT'S IN A NAPPY?
Babies' stools can be very brightly coloured, greenish at first, then probably yellow or orange, or greyish green if your baby is bottlefed. Breastfed babies have quite runny stools. Bottle-fed babies' stools are firmer and smellier.

Some babies fill their nappies at or around every feed. Some, especially breastfed babies, can go for several days, even a week, without a bowel movement. Either is normal. Quite a lot of babies also strain or even cry when passing a stool. This is also normal. Your baby's not constipated if the stools are soft.

From day to day or week to week, your baby's stools will probably vary a bit. But if you notice a marked change of any kind, such as the stools becoming very smelly or very watery or becoming hard, particularly if there's blood in them, you should talk to your doctor or health visitor.

Things to ask your GP or health visitor
It'll help if you can keep a note of just how long, and how often, your baby cries over a few days. That way your GP or health visitor can see what the problem is. Then you could ask:
- Is my baby physically well?
- (If you bottle feed) Should I change the formula?
- (If you breastfeed) Should I change my diet?
- Is there any medication that could help?

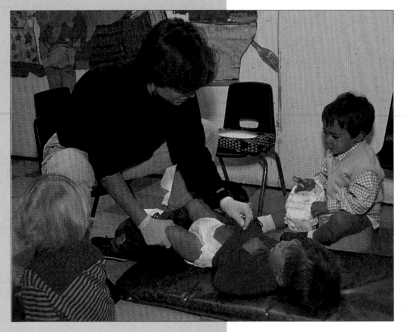

NAPPY CHANGING

Some babies have very delicate skin and need changing the minute they wet themselves if they're not to get sore and red. Others seem to be tougher and get along fine with a change before or after every feed. All babies need to be changed when they're dirty to prevent nappy rash and because they smell awful!

GETTING ORGANISED

- Get everything you need for changing in one place before you start. The best place to change a nappy is on a changing mat or towel on the floor, particularly if you've more than one baby. If you sit down you won't hurt your back and, as your baby gets bigger, he or she can't wriggle off and hurt him or herself. If you're using a changing table, keep one hand on your baby at all times.
- Make sure you've a supply of nappies. If you're using terries, ask a friend, or your midwife, to show you how to fold and pin them. Experiment to find out what suits you best.
- You'll need a supply of cotton wool and a bowl of warm water or baby lotion, or baby wipes.
- Make sure you've a spare set of clothes. In the early weeks you often need to change everything.

GETTING STARTED

- If your baby is dirty, use the nappy to clean off most of it. Then, using the cotton wool and warm water or baby lotion, clean girls from front to back to avoid getting germs into the vagina. Boys should be cleaned around the penis and testicles (balls). Don't pull back the foreskin when cleaning the penis. It's just as important to clean carefully when you're changing a wet nappy.
- You can use a barrier cream such as zinc and castor oil, which helps to protect against nappy rash, but it's usually enough just to leave your baby's skin clean and dry – and some babies are sensitive to these creams.
- Avoid using baby powder because it can make your baby choke.
- If you're using a terry nappy, fold it, put in a nappy liner if you wish, pin it with a proper nappy pin that won't spring open, and put on or tie on plastic pants.
- If you're using disposable nappies, take care not to get water or cream on the sticky tabs or they won't stick.

Nappy rash

Most babies get nappy rash at some time. There may be red spots or just general soreness. To protect your baby against nappy rash:
- change your baby's nappy often.
- keep your baby's skin clean and dry (see pages 23–25 for how to clean your baby). If you use soap, carefully rinse it all off because it can overdry the skin.
- leave your baby to kick for a while without a nappy on if the room is warm enough, so that your baby's skin gets some fresh air.
If the rash gets very bad or won't go away, ask your health visitor or GP about it. Your baby may have thrush, which is an infection that needs treatment. Your GP can prescribe a cream that will clear up such an infection quite quickly. Sometimes medicine may be needed as well.

NAPPY HYGIENE

Dispose of the dirty nappy. Put as much of the contents as you can down the toilet. If you're using terries with disposable liners the liner can be flushed away, but don't ever flush a nappy down the toilet, because you'll block it.

Disposable nappies can be rolled up and resealed with the tabs. Put them in a plastic bag kept only for nappies, then tie it up and keep it outside by your bin.

Terries must be washed and sterilised. You'll need a plastic bucket with a lid, which must be refilled every day with clean water and sterilising powder made up to the manufacturer's instructions. Each nappy must be soaked in the steriliser following the instructions and then a load can be washed every day. Use very hot water and avoid enzyme washing powders and fabric conditioners, which can irritate your baby's skin. Make sure the nappies are very well rinsed.

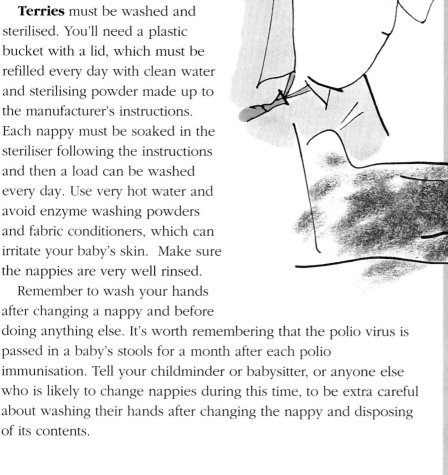

Remember to wash your hands after changing a nappy and before doing anything else. It's worth remembering that the polio virus is passed in a baby's stools for a month after each polio immunisation. Tell your childminder or babysitter, or anyone else who is likely to change nappies during this time, to be extra careful about washing their hands after changing the nappy and disposing of its contents.

WASHING AND BATHING

WASHING

Wash your baby's face, neck, hands, and bottom carefully every day. Choose a time when your baby is awake and contented and make sure the room is warm. Organise everything you need in advance: a bowl of warm water, a towel, cotton wool, a fresh nappy, and, if necessary, clean clothes.

● Hold your baby on your knee, or lie your baby on a changing mat, and take off all your baby's clothes except for a vest and nappy. Then wrap your baby in the towel.

- Dip the cotton wool in the water (not too much) and wipe gently around your baby's eyes from the nose outward, using a fresh piece of cotton wool for each eye.
- Using a fresh piece of cotton wool, clean around your baby's ears, but don't clean inside them.
- Wash the rest of your baby's face, neck, and hands the same way and dry them gently with the towel.
- Now change your baby's nappy as described on page 22.

In the first ten days you should also clean around your baby's navel each day. Your midwife will show you how.

BATHING

Bathing two or three times a week is quite enough, but you can do it daily if your baby enjoys it. Don't bath your baby straight after a feed or when your baby is hungry or tired. Make sure the room is warm.

Have everything you need at hand: a baby bath or washing up bowl filled with warm water, two towels (in case of accidents!), baby bath liquid (avoid this if your baby has particularly dry skin) or baby soap, a clean nappy, clean clothes, and cotton wool.

- Make sure the water is warm, not hot; check it with your wrist or elbow.
- Hold your baby on your knee and follow the instructions given above for cleaning his or her face.
- Wash your baby's hair with baby soap or liquid, then rinse carefully, supporting your baby over the bowl. Dry gently.

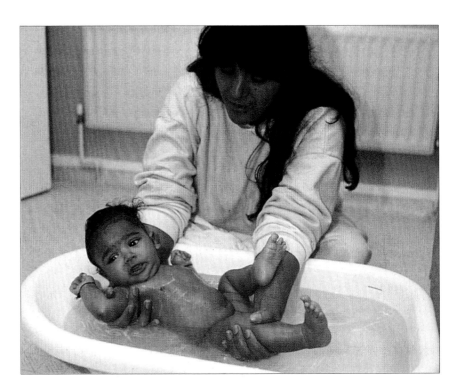

- Now remove your baby's nappy, wiping away any mess. If you're using baby soap, soap your baby all over (avoiding his or her face) while still on your knee, keeping a firm grip while you do so.

- Lower your baby gently into the bowl, using one hand to hold your baby's upper arm and support his or her head and shoulders; keep your baby's head clear of the water. Use the other hand to gently swish the water over your baby without splashing. Never leave your baby alone in the bath; not even for a second.
- Lift your baby out and pat dry, paying special attention to the creases. You may want to use this time to massage baby oil into your baby's skin. Many babies love this and it may help your baby relax and sleep. Lay your baby on a towel on the floor as both the baby – and your hands – might be a bit slippery.

If your baby seems frightened of bathing and cries, you could try bathing together, but make sure the water is not too hot. It's easier if someone else holds your baby while you get in and out.

TAKING YOUR BABY OUT

Your baby is ready to go out as soon as you feel fit enough to go yourself.

WALKING
Walking is good for both of you. It may be easiest to take a tiny baby in a sling. If you use a buggy make sure your baby can lie down with his or her back flat.

IN A CAR
It's illegal for anyone to hold a baby while sitting in the front seat of a car. The only safe way for your baby to travel in a car is in a properly secured, backward-facing, baby seat, or in a carry cot (not a Moses basket) with the cover on and secured with special straps.

Some areas have special loan schemes to enable you to borrow a suitable baby seat when you and your baby first return from hospital. Ask your midwife or health visitor.

If you have a car with air bags in the front your baby should *not* travel in the front seat (even facing backwards) because of the danger of suffocation if the bag inflates.

IN COLD WEATHER
Make sure your baby is wrapped up warm in cold weather because babies chill very easily. Take the extra clothing *off* when you get into a warm place so that your baby doesn't then overheat.

IN HOT WEATHER
Keep babies less than one year old out of the sun. And older children should always be protected, either by covering them up or with a high protection sunscreen (sun protection factor 15+). Babies' and children's skin burns easily, even in sun which wouldn't affect your own skin.

TWINS (OR MORE)

Parents who've only one child often think that having two together is much the same sort of experience, but doubled. If you've twins, you'll know differently. Caring for twins, or more, is very different from caring for two of different ages. There's certainly a lot more work, and often you've to find different ways of doing things.

You need as much support as you can get. If you've more than two babies you may be able to get a home help from your local council. Find out what their policy is. A few hours of help with housework a week could make a big difference. If your council doesn't provide home helps, ask your health visitor if she has any suggestions.

You may get a lot of help from family and friends, but it also helps to be in contact with other parents of twins. The Twins and Multiple Births Association (address on page 136) offers a lot of helpful information, including information about local Twins Clubs. Through these clubs you can meet other parents whose experiences are like yours, and get support and practical advice. Often you can get secondhand equipment too, such as twin prams and buggies.

How your child will grow

2

Your baby may walk at 11 months. Your neighbour's baby may still be crawling at 16 months. Both are quite normal. One child may be talking in sentences at two years old, another may've just started to put two words together. Both are normal. Each child is different because each is an individual. This chapter looks at the way children grow.

HOW CHILDREN DEVELOP

Children aren't just born different, they also have different lives and they'll learn different things. A child who plays a lot with toys will be learning to use his or her hands and eyes together. A child who goes out to the park every day will soon learn the names of ducks and trees. A child who is often talked to will learn more words. A child who's given love and praise for learning new things will want to learn more.

Some children have difficulty learning, perhaps because of physical problems with, for example, hearing or seeing. You may already know that your child's development is likely to be slower than normal or you may be worried about your child's progress. Your child may be offered regular development reviews (see page 33) but you don't have to wait for a check-up. If you're concerned, talk to your health visitor or GP. If something's holding your child back, the sooner you find out, the sooner you can do something to help. For more on this see page 37. For more about play and learning see pages 39–44.

(A father) "When he does something new that he's never done before, that's magic. It's like no other baby in the world has ever done it."

"My mum said 'Isn't she walking yet?' And as it happened, the little boy next door who's about the same age was up and walking, and Annie was just sitting there not doing a thing. My mum said I was walking at that age. She kept going on about it."

(A father) "I want to know that she's all right and, you know, keeping up."

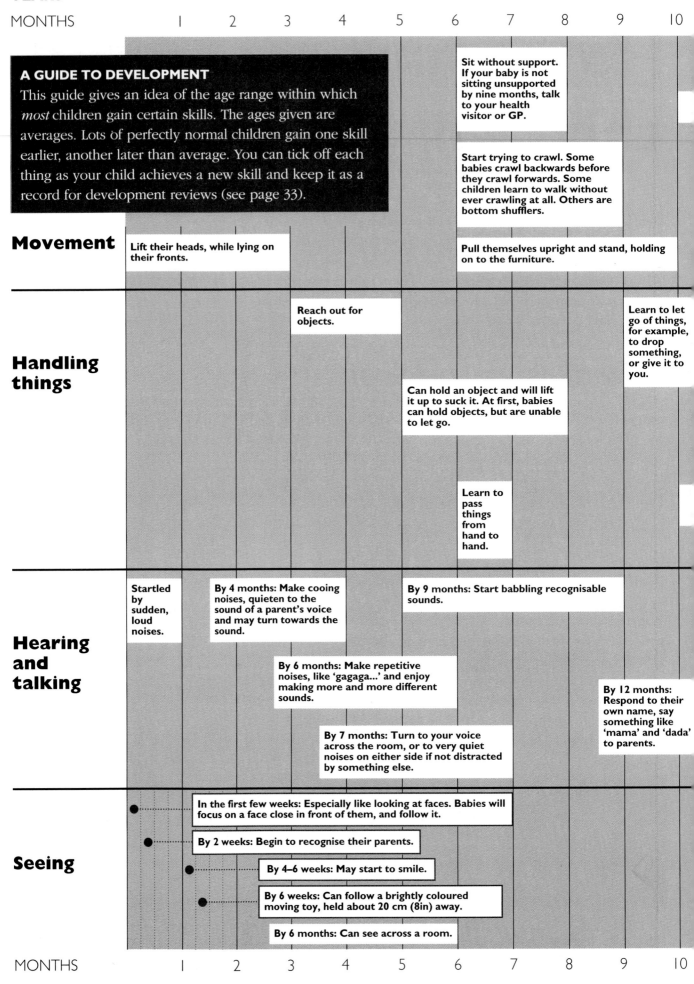

YEARS

MONTHS | 1 | 2 | 3 | 4 | 5 | 6 | 7 | 8 | 9 | 10

A GUIDE TO DEVELOPMENT

This guide gives an idea of the age range within which *most* children gain certain skills. The ages given are averages. Lots of perfectly normal children gain one skill earlier, another later than average. You can tick off each thing as your child achieves a new skill and keep it as a record for development reviews (see page 33).

Movement

Lift their heads, while lying on their fronts.

Sit without support. If your baby is not sitting unsupported by nine months, talk to your health visitor or GP.

Start trying to crawl. Some babies crawl backwards before they crawl forwards. Some children learn to walk without ever crawling at all. Others are bottom shufflers.

Pull themselves upright and stand, holding on to the furniture.

Handling things

Reach out for objects.

Can hold an object and will lift it up to suck it. At first, babies can hold objects, but are unable to let go.

Learn to pass things from hand to hand.

Learn to let go of things, for example, to drop something, or give it to you.

Hearing and talking

Startled by sudden, loud noises.

By 4 months: Make cooing noises, quieten to the sound of a parent's voice and may turn towards the sound.

By 6 months: Make repetitive noises, like 'gagaga...' and enjoy making more and more different sounds.

By 7 months: Turn to your voice across the room, or to very quiet noises on either side if not distracted by something else.

By 9 months: Start babbling recognisable sounds.

By 12 months: Respond to their own name, say something like 'mama' and 'dada' to parents.

Seeing

In the first few weeks: Especially like looking at faces. Babies will focus on a face close in front of them, and follow it.

By 2 weeks: Begin to recognise their parents.

By 4–6 weeks: May start to smile.

By 6 weeks: Can follow a brightly coloured moving toy, held about 20 cm (8in) away.

By 6 months: Can see across a room.

MONTHS | 1 | 2 | 3 | 4 | 5 | 6 | 7 | 8 | 9 | 10

YEARS

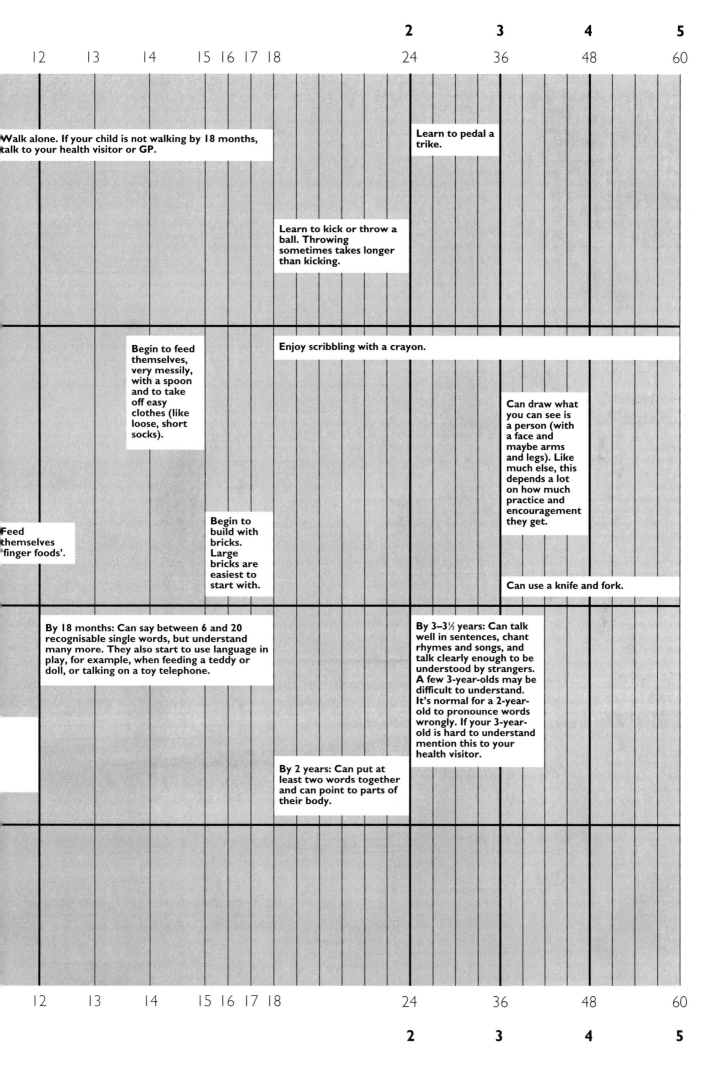

12   13   14   15 16 17 18   24   36   48   60

Walk alone. If your child is not walking by 18 months, talk to your health visitor or GP.

Learn to pedal a trike.

Learn to kick or throw a ball. Throwing sometimes takes longer than kicking.

Begin to feed themselves, very messily, with a spoon and to take off easy clothes (like loose, short socks).

Enjoy scribbling with a crayon.

Can draw what you can see is a person (with a face and maybe arms and legs). Like much else, this depends a lot on how much practice and encouragement they get.

Feed themselves 'finger foods'.

Begin to build with bricks. Large bricks are easiest to start with.

Can use a knife and fork.

By 18 months: Can say between 6 and 20 recognisable single words, but understand many more. They also start to use language in play, for example, when feeding a teddy or doll, or talking on a toy telephone.

By 3–3½ years: Can talk well in sentences, chant rhymes and songs, and talk clearly enough to be understood by strangers. A few 3-year-olds may be difficult to understand. It's normal for a 2-year-old to pronounce words wrongly. If your 3-year-old is hard to understand mention this to your health visitor.

By 2 years: Can put at least two words together and can point to parts of their body.

FEET – AND FIRST SHOES

Babies' and small children's feet grow very fast and it's important that the bones grow straight.

- The bones in a baby's toes are soft at birth. If they're cramped by tight bootees, socks, stretch suits, or pram shoes, the toes can't straighten out and grow properly. So keep your baby's feet as free as possible. Make sure bootees and socks leave room for their toes, both in length and width. If the feet of a stretch suit become too small, cut them off and use socks instead.
- Don't put your child into proper shoes until he or she can walk alone and keep them only for walking outside at first.
- When you buy shoes, it's best to have your child's feet measured. Shoes should be about 1 cm (a bit less than ½") beyond the longest toe and wide enough for all the toes to lie flat.
- 'Multi-fit' shoes, which you buy in chain stores or mail order, are cheaper, but only come in one width fitting. They fit only about half of all British children – those who are D or E fitting. If you buy these shoes, or get shoes secondhand, check carefully that they fit. Make sure there's plenty of room for your child's toes, and also that the shoe isn't too loose. Don't use secondhand shoes with misshapen soles.
- Shoes with a lace, buckle or velcro fastening hold the heel in place and stop the foot slipping forward and damaging the toes. If the heel of a shoe slips off when your child stands on tiptoe, it doesn't fit.
- It's better to buy cheap shoes, and throw them away as soon as they're worn out, than expensive ones that you can't afford to replace often enough. Have your child's feet measured for each new pair.
- Check that socks are the right size.
- Most minor foot problems in children correct themselves spontaneously.
- If you've any worry to do with your child's feet, see your GP or health visitor. Your GP can refer you to a chiropodist, orthopaedic surgeon or paediatric physiotherapist if necessary.

TEETH

The time when babies get their first primary teeth (milk teeth) varies. A few are born with a tooth already through. Others have no teeth at one year old. Most get their first tooth at around six months, usually in front and at the bottom. Most have all their primary teeth by about two and a half. The first (permanent) second teeth come through at the back at around the age of six.

There are 20 primary (first) teeth in all, ten at the top, ten at the bottom.

How to check the length of your child's shoes

- Cut two thin strips of cardboard. Get your child to stand on them in bare feet.

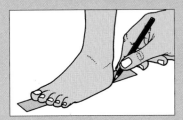

- Mark your child's longest toe and the back of his or her heel.
- Cut the cardboard at the marks.

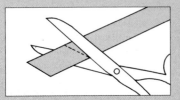

- Slip the strips into your child's shoes so that one end touches the toe of the shoe.
- If the shoe fits, there should be a 1 cm gap between the end of the cardboard strip and the heel of your child's shoe. If there is less than a 1 cm gap, if the cardboard strip touches the heel, or if it doesn't lie flat, then the shoe is too short. This is just a rough guide. If you can, have shoes fitted or checked by a trained shoe fitter.

TEETHING

Some teeth come through with no pain or trouble at all. At other times you may notice that the gum is sore and red where the tooth is coming, or that one cheek is flushed. Your baby may dribble, gnaw, and chew a lot, or just be fretful, but it's often hard to tell whether this is really due to teething.

It can help to give your baby something hard to chew on such as a teething ring, or a dried crust of bread, or a scrubbed carrot (stay nearby in case of choking). Avoid rusks because almost all contain some sugar. Constant chewing and sucking on sugary things can cause bad tooth decay, even if your baby has only one or two teeth.

For babies over four months old you can try teething gel rubbed on the gum. You can get this from the pharmacist. Follow the instructions on the packet. It's possible to get sugar-free teething gel. For younger babies you should talk to your GP. You may also want to give baby paracetemol. Follow the instructions on the bottle for your child's age, or check with your pharmacist or GP.

People put all sorts of things down to teething – rashes, crying, bad temper, runny noses, extra dirty nappies. But be careful not to explain away what might be the signs of illness by saying it's 'just teething'.

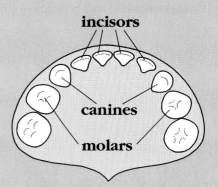

CARING FOR YOUR CHILD'S TEETH

- Keep down the number of times each day that your child eats or drinks something sugary.
- Brush your child's teeth and gums thoroughly, twice each day, using a pea-sized amount of fluoride toothpaste; help an older child. Let your child see you brushing your teeth too.

Cutting down on sugar

Sugar causes tooth decay. It's not just the amount of sugar in sweet food and drinks that matters, but perhaps more importantly, how often there are sugary things in the mouth. This is why sweet drinks in a bottle, and lollipops, are so bad. The teeth are bathed in sugar over quite a long time.

- **From the time you start your baby on foods and drinks other than milk, avoid giving sweet things.** Try to encourage savoury tastes. Watch for the sugar in baby foods in tins and packets (even the savoury varieties), and rusks; and in baby drinks, especially fizzy drinks, squash, and syrups.
- **Try not to give your child sweet foods and drinks more than three times a day.** You could try keeping them for meals only. If you can cut down even more, all the better.
- **Try to find treats other than biscuits or sweets**, and ask relatives and friends to do the same. Use things like stickers, badges, hair slides, crayons, small books, notebooks and colouring books, soap, and bubble baths. These may be more expensive than one small sweet, but they all last longer, and maybe it is no bad thing if treats happen less often.

Fluoride
Fluoride is a chemical which helps prevent tooth decay. In a few areas, it's naturally present in the water supply, and in others, it's added. It's also added to most toothpastes. If you live in an area without fluoride in the water supply, you could talk to your health visitor and/or dentist about fluoride supplements. These come as drops (for babies) and tablets (for older children). You can buy them from the pharmacist.

It is possible to give too much fluoride – which can badly discolour teeth. So don't give supplements and use fluoride toothpaste together. Ask your doctor, dentist or health visitor before giving supplements. There may be sufficient fluoride in the water supply already.

- **If children are given sweets or chocolate, it's less harmful for their teeth if they eat them all at once** than if they eat, say, a little every hour or so.
- **Be aware of the amount of sugar the whole family's eating.** Look for ways of cutting down. See page 75 for some suggestions.
- **Avoid giving bedtime drinks** unless you can clean your child's teeth before he or she falls asleep.

BRUSHING YOUR CHILD'S TEETH

- **Start early, as soon as your baby's teeth start to come through.** Buy a baby toothbrush and use it with a pea-sized blob of fluoride toothpaste. You don't have to use a baby toothpaste. Some children do seem happier with the milder taste, but it's much more expensive. Don't worry if you don't manage to brush much at first. The important thing at the start is to get tooth brushing accepted as part of every day routine. That's why it's important you do it too.
- **Gradually start to brush your child's teeth more thoroughly, brushing all the surfaces of all the teeth.** Do it twice a day – just before bed, and whatever other time in the day fits in best. Not many children like having their teeth brushed, so you may have to work at it a bit. Try not to let it become a battle. If it becomes difficult, try games, or try brushing your own teeth at the same time and then helping your child to 'finish off'.
- **Go on helping your child to brush until you're sure he or she is brushing well enough.** You'll probably have to keep an eye on your child's tooth brushing until he or she is a teenager.

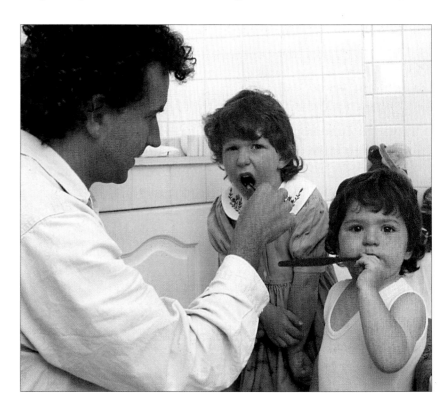

Taking your child to the dentist

You can take your child to be registered with a dentist under the NHS as soon as your child has been born – even before any teeth come through. Your dentist can give advice on your child's oral health. NHS dental treatment for children is free.

Take your child with you when you go to the dentist, so that going to the dentist becomes a normal event.

If you need to find a dentist, you can ask at your local clinic or contact your family health services authority (FHSA) – the address and telephone number will be in the phone book.

KEEPING AN EYE ON YOUR BABY'S GROWTH AND DEVELOPMENT

PARENT-HELD RECORDS

In most clinics now you'll be given a Personal Child Health Record or parent-held record for your baby. This is a way of keeping track of your child's progress. It makes sure that, wherever you are and whatever happens to your child, you'll have a copy of the records for your own information and for health professionals when and where you may need it.

To start with you'll want to use the records mainly to record your child's height and weight. Then you can add information about immunisations (see page 90), childhood illness, and accidents. These records are quite new and health visitors or doctors may not always remember to fill them in. It's important to remind them to do so, so that there's a full record of your child's health.

DEVELOPMENT REVIEWS

Your GP and health visitors will offer you regular development reviews. These used to be called development checks, but they've recently been changed. The review gives you, the parents, an opportunity to say what you've noticed about your child. You can also discuss anything at all that may concern you about your child's health and general behaviour. Not just the big things, but the kinds of worries and niggles that every parent has but feels unsure about taking to a doctor or nurse.

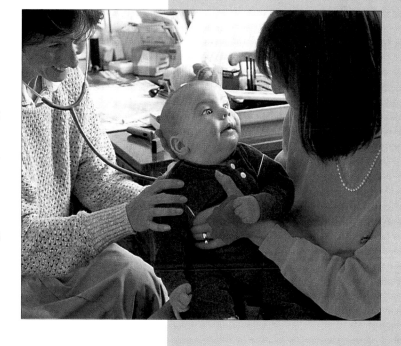

The review programme

Development reviews will usually be carried out by your health visitor, sometimes alone and sometimes with a doctor. They may be carried out at a regular clinic session or in your own home. The aim is to spot any problems as early as possible so that, if necessary, some action can be taken. So even if you think your child is doing fine it's worth having the review. Your health visitor will tell you when it's due, but if you're concerned about something at any other time, don't wait. Ask to see someone. You can expect to be invited to a development review when your child is:

- 6 to 8 weeks old.
- 6 to 9 months old.
- 18 to 24 months old.
- 3 to 4½ years old.

You may also be offered one just after your child starts school.

HEIGHT AND WEIGHT

Your child's height and weight are a very useful guide to general progress and development. You can have your baby regularly weighed at your child health clinic or doctor's baby clinic. Older children should be weighed and measured as part of other health checks. Babies vary in how fast they put on weight, but usually weight gain is quickest in the first six to nine months, and then slows.

- Most babies double their birthweight by 4–5 months.
- Most babies treble their birthweight by a year.

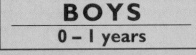

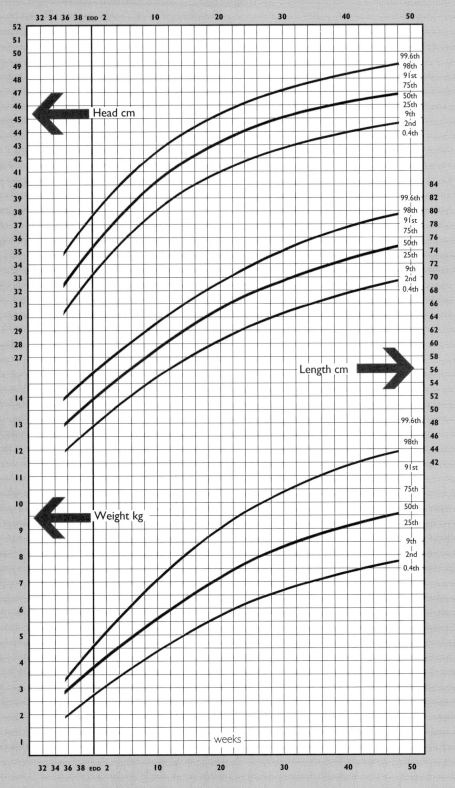

Boys and girls have different charts because boys are on average heavier and taller and their growth pattern is slightly different.

The middle centile line ('the 50th centile', drawn as a red line on these charts) shows the average weight and growth of white children, but your child's weight and growth might lie anywhere between the blue centile lines. If your child's height and weight always fall outside these lines, or veers upward or downward from the printed centile, talk to your health visitor or GP.

If your baby is premature, plot the height, weight and head size details from the week in your pregnancy when your baby was born. If the birth was in the 36th week of pregnancy your child should reach the 10 week point on the chart when 14 weeks old.

Some weeks your baby will gain weight; some weeks he or she will not gain weight. This doesn't matter. What's looked for is a general weight gain over a period of weeks.

Understanding your child's height and weight chart

Your child's growth will be recorded on 'centile' charts so that his or her progress can be easily followed. Boys and girls have different charts because boys are on average heavier and taller and their growth pattern is slightly different. Page 34 shows an example of a boy's height, weight and head size centile lines for babies up to one year old; this page shows a girl's height and weight centile lines for children from one to five.

New charts were produced in October 1993 based on the latest information about child growth. However, some clinics may still be using the old ones which are based on out-of-date information.

The centile lines printed on the charts show roughly the kind of growth expected in weight and in length. On each of the charts the middle line (shown as a red line in this book) represents the national average for white British babies. For example, if 100 babies are weighed and measured, 50 will weigh and measure more than the amount indicated by the red line, and 50 will weigh and measure less.

Most babies' and children's weight and height will fall between the two centile lines coloured blue in this book. Only two out of every 100 babies and children will have weights and heights that fall outside these centiles.

These data are based on the average heights and weights of white children. It's worth bearing in mind that if you're of Asian origin your baby will on average be lighter and if you're of Afro-Caribbean origin your baby will on average be heavier and longer.

Your child's height and weight (and head size if under a year) will be plotted as a curved line on one of these charts. This makes it easy to see how your child is developing.

Whatever weight and length your baby is at birth, he or she should have a fairly steady growth, resulting in a line curving in roughly the same way, and usually inside, the centile lines on the chart.

During the first two years of life it is quite usual for a baby's line to cross the centiles on the chart from time to time, but if at any time your baby's weight line suddenly goes up or drops (and it may drop, for example, because of illness), talk to your health visitor or GP about it. You should also talk to your health visitor or GP if, after the age of two, your baby's height curve does not follow a centile line or starts to veer upwards or downwards from it.

GIRLS
1 – 5 years

General development

Some health visitors may ask your child to do little tasks such as building with blocks or identifying pictures. Others may simply watch your child playing or perhaps drawing, and get an idea from her observation, and your comments, of how your child is doing. If you look at the development chart on pages 28–9 you'll have an idea of the kind of physical and verbal skills they're looking for. If your child's first language isn't English, you may need to ask if development reviews can be carried out with the help of someone who can speak your child's language. See page 124 for information about linkworkers.

If your child seems slow in one particular area of development you'll have the opportunity to discuss what the reason may be. And to see whether there's anything useful that needs to be done to speed things up.

Eyesight

You can see from the chart on pages 28–9 that a baby should be able to see from birth. Eyesight develops gradually over the next six months.

By the first review, you'll have noticed whether or not your baby can follow a colourful object held about eight inches away with his or her eyes. If this isn't happening you should mention it.

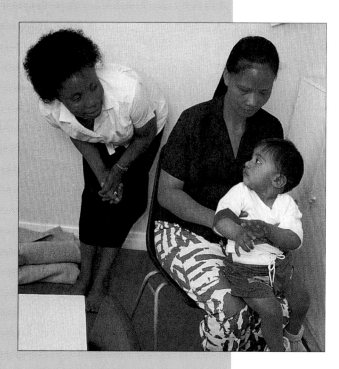

At birth a baby's eyes may roll away from each other occasionally. If a baby is squinting all, or much, of the time tell your health visitor and your GP.

If your baby is squinting you'll need to be referred to an orthoptist or ophthalmologist who specialises in understanding children's eyes.

Hearing and talking

Hearing and talking are linked. If your child can't hear properly he or she'll have great difficulty learning to talk and may need to be taught other ways of communicating. So the sooner hearing problems are discovered the greater the chance that something can be done. See pages 28–9 to find out how you can check if your child can hear.

It isn't only hearing that is important though. Babies don't learn to talk unless they're talked to, even if, at first, the conversation is limited to making noises at each other. By learning to take it in turns to make babbling noises, your baby is learning what a conversation feels like. Most parents quite naturally join in babbling sessions with their babies and so they're very often the first people to notice if there's a problem.

If you're ever worried about your child's language development, talk to your GP or health visitor. Your child may be helped by referral to a speech therapist.

Your baby's hearing may be tested at birth in the hospital. No baby is 'too young' for a hearing assessment.

You should expect a hearing assessment at six to nine months. If there's no apparent problem, but you're still worried, ask for another appointment. If a problem is found, your baby will need to have a follow up assessment because hearing loss may be temporary, due to a cold or a passing infection.

If your child doesn't seem to hear properly at the second appointment, or you are still worried, ask for a referral to a specialist.

CHILDREN WITH SPECIAL NEEDS

For some families, everything is not 'all right'. Sometimes what begins as a worry does turn out to be a more serious problem or disability.

If this happens to you, your first need will be for information about the problem and what it's likely to mean for your child and for you. You'll have a lot of questions (see box below). Put them all to your GP, your health visitor, and to specialists to whom you are referred.

Be determined and persist if you need to. Not all health professionals talk easily or well to parents. And you yourself may find it's difficult to hear and take in all that's said to you, first, or even second time round. Rather than live with unanswered questions, go back and ask again for the information or opinion you feel you need. Make a list of the questions you want to ask before you see the health visitor, GP or specialist. Or you could take along a tape recorder. If in the end the honest answer is 'I don't know' or 'We're not sure', that's better than no answer at all.

HELP FOR CHILDREN WITH SPECIAL NEEDS
Child development centres
In some areas, teams of professionals (doctors, therapists, health visitors, social workers), usually working from what is known as a child development centre, are available to help support children with special needs and their families. You can be referred to such a team through your GP or health visitor.

Voluntary organisations
You can also get information, advice, and support from organisations dealing with particular handicaps, illnesses, and other problems. Through them, you can often contact other parents in situations like your own. See pages 134–5 for the names and addresses of some organisations that might be able to help.

Bilingual children
Children who're growing up in a family who speak more than one language don't usually have problems. A few develop language more slowly. The important thing is to talk to your child in whatever language feels comfortable to you. This may mean one parent using one language and the other using another. Children usually adapt to this.

Some questions you may like to ask
● Is there a name for my child's problem? If so, what is it?
● Are more tests needed to get a clear diagnosis or confirm what's been found out?
● Is it likely to get better or likely to get worse, or will it stay roughly the same?
● Where is the best place to go for medical help?
● Where is the best place to go for practical help?
● How can I get in touch with other parents who have children with a similar problem?
● How can I find out how best to help my child?

Specialist help

There are many services available to help children who've special needs to learn and develop: for example, physiotherapy, speech therapy, occupational therapy, home learning schemes, play groups, opportunity groups, nurseries, and nursery schools and classes. To find out what's available in your area, ask your health visitor, GP, social services department, or the educational adviser for special needs at your local education department. See pages 122–5 for more information about the services, including information about regional variations.

Special needs assessment

Local education authorities who think a child over two years old may have special educational needs must make an assessment of his or her needs. For a child under two an assessment must be made if a parent asks for it. This assessment is a way of getting advice about your child's educational needs. You can take part in the assessment yourself. The Advisory Centre for Education (see page 134) offers advice on education and produces a handbook on the subject.

Benefits advice

For information about social security benefits for children with special needs, see page 132. See also 'Help with national health service costs' page 131.

Learning and playing

3

What we call playing is really the way our children learn. With toys and their imaginations they practise all the skills they'll need as they grow up. The more they play, the more they learn and the best thing about it is that they love it.

PLAYING WITH YOU

Young children find it hard to play alone. They need attention from someone who can play with them. Gradually they'll learn to entertain themselves for some of the time, but first they need to learn how to do that.

In the meantime, you can't spend all your time playing. You've other things to do and other people to attend to. Fortunately children learn from everything that's going on around them, and everything they do. When you're washing up, your toddler can stand next to you on a chair and wash the saucepan lids; when you cook, make sure your baby can see and talk to you as you work.

The times when they're not learning much are the times when they're bored. That's as true for babies as of older children. So what really matters?

● Find a lot of different things for your child to look at, think about, and do (see 'Ideas for play' page 40).

● Make what you're doing fun and interesting for your child, so you can get it done.

● Make some time to give all your attention to what your child wants to do.

● Talk about anything and everything, even about the washing up or what to put on the shopping list, so that you share as much as possible.

● Find a place and time when your child can learn how to use his or her body by running, jumping and climbing. This is especially important if you don't have much room at home.

● Find other people who can spend time with your child at those times when you really do need to attend to something else.

"I'd play with them all the time if I could. I tell you, it's much more fun than doing the housework."

"There are things I've got to do. She's forever asking me to play, and I'm forever saying 'in a minute, in a minute'."

"I don't know that we play all that much. We do a lot of things together, but it's often the shopping, and hanging out the washing, and that sort of thing. It may not be play, but we have a good time."

Ideas for play

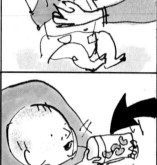

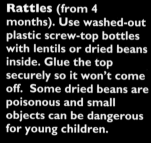

Rattles (from 4 months). Use washed-out plastic screw-top bottles with lentils or dried beans inside. Glue the top securely so it won't come off. Some dried beans are poisonous and small objects can be dangerous for young children.

Play dough (from about 18 months). Put 1 cup of water, 1 cup of plain flour, 2 tbs of cream of tartar, ½ cup of salt, 1tbs of cooking oil, and some food colouring or powder paint in a pan. Stir over a medium heat until this makes a dough. Cool. Store in a plastic box in the fridge.

Junk modelling (30 months). Collect all sorts of cardboard boxes, cartons, yoghurt pots, milk bottle tops – anything – and some children's glue, strong enough to glue cardboard, but not to mark clothes. The sort with a brush is easiest to use.

Pretend cooking (from 18 months). Use a bowl, spoons for measuring out and mixing small quantities of 'real' ingredients (flour, lentils, rice, sugar, custard powder) and put out in egg cups or bowls. Use water to mix.

Television gives your child a lot of entertainment, and you a bit of peace. It gives you more peace if it's not on all the time. Make sure you know what your child's watching. And watch with your child when you can so you can talk about what you see.

Playing with water is fun for all ages: in the bath, sink, a plastic bowl, paddling pool. Use plastic bottles for pouring and squirting, plastic tubing, sponge, colander, straws, funnel, spoons – anything unbreakable. Remember never to leave a young child alone with water.

Dressing up (from 18 months). Collect old hats, bags, gloves, scarves, nighties, lengths of material, tea towels, old curtains. Ask friends, relatives or try jumble sales. Paper plates or cut up cereal packets make good masks – cut slits for the eyes and tie on with string.

Reading. Even quite small babies like looking at picture books. Local libraries usually have a good range of children's books and sometimes run story sessions for young children.

Drawing and painting (from 18 months). Use with crayons, felt tips, powder paint. Add washing-up liquid and water to powder paint for a thicker paint. You can use old envelopes slit open and the inside of cereal packets for paper.

Walking. Encourage your child to walk with you (using reins for safety) as soon as he or she is able. It may be slower, but children need exercise, and so do you!

MAKING TIME

Some things do have to happen at certain times, and your child does slowly have to learn about that. But when you're with your child try not to work to a strict timetable. Your child is unlikely to fit in with it and then you both get frustrated. A lot can be pushed around to suit the mood of you and your child. There's no rule that says the washing-up has to be done before you go to the playground, especially if the sun's shining and your child's bursting with energy.

KEEP YOUR CHILD FIT

Children want to use their bodies to practise until they learn how to crawl, walk, run, jump and climb. The more opportunity you can give them, the happier they'll be and you'll probably find that they sleep better and are more cheerful and easy going when they've had the opportunity to run off some energy. At the same time you'll be helping their muscle development and general fitness and, if they start to see outdoor activities and sports as a part of their lives, you'll be laying down the habits that will keep them fitter as adults. Make time for your children to exercise.

- Allow your baby to lie and kick his or her legs.
- Make your floor a safe place for a crawler to move around.
- Make time for your toddler to walk with you rather than using the buggy.
- Take toddlers and young children to the park to try climbing and swinging or just so that they have a safe space to run.
- Find out what's on for parents and babies at the local leisure centre.
- Take your baby swimming – wait until he or she is five months old (after immunisation).

HOW TO MAKE SURE YOUR CHILD LEARNS WHAT YOU WANT HIM OR HER TO LEARN

When children play they're learning what they want. Often they'll also be the things you want them to learn, but for some things they may need extra encouragement, like using the potty (see page 51), washing, or dressing themselves, learning what not to touch, and where it's not safe to run. It's worth thinking about how you do it.

- **Wait until you think your child's ready.** Forcing something too soon usually ends in failure. You get cross and upset, your child gets cross and upset, and the whole thing becomes impossible. If it doesn't work out, leave it for a few weeks and try again.

- **Try not to make it seem too important.** Your child may learn to eat with a spoon because it's fun, but still want to be fed when he or she is tired, or may enjoy the first few times on the potty because you're so pleased, and then get bored with the idea. In time he or she'll see that it is worthwhile learning to be more grown up and independent.

- **Keep it safe.** If your child's under three years old he or she can't really understand why not to touch your stereo or pull leaves off your pot plants, so keep things you don't want touched well out of the way and you'll both be less frustrated. Time enough to learn about not touching when your child can understand why.

- **Be encouraging.** Your happiness is your child's best reward for good behaviour. If you give your child a big smile, a cuddle, or praise when he or she does something right your child is much more likely to try doing it again. Giving your child attention and praise for doing something right works much better than telling him or her off for doing something wrong.

- **Don't ask for perfection, or for instant success.** It's safest to expect everything to take much longer than you'd hoped.

- **Set an example.** Whatever it may look like, your child does want to be like you and do what you do. So seeing you wash in the bath, brush your teeth, or use the toilet does help.

- **Avoid fuss and confrontation.** Once something gets blown up, it can take longer and be much more difficult for everybody to calm down.

- **Be firm.** Children need you to decide some things for them, and need you to stick to your decisions. They need some firm guidelines. So try not to waver. You might start something like potty training, decide your child isn't ready, and give up for a while. That's fine. But a child who is in nappies one day, out the next, back in them the next, is bound to get confused.
- **Be consistent.** For the same reason, it's important that everybody involved in looking after your child is teaching more or less the same things in more or less the same way. If you and your partner, or you and your childminder, do things very differently, your child won't learn so easily, and may well play you off against each other.
- **Do what's right for your child, for you, and for the way you live.** It doesn't matter what the child next door can or can't do. Don't compete; don't ask your child to compete.

No parent is perfect and some children seem to find these lessons particularly difficult to learn. See pages 57–63 for dealing with difficult behaviour.

MAKING FRIENDS

Learning how to make friends is one of the most important things your child will do. If your child learns early how to get on well with others he or she will get off to a better start at school, and a happy child learns better than a child who's anxious and afraid of others.

It's never too soon to start, especially if yours is an only child. Even babies and small children like other children's company, although at first they play alongside each other rather than with each other. Ask your health visitor if there's a new parents group meeting in your area.

As your child starts to crawl and walk you could try a parent and toddler group or 'one o'clock club'. These can be great for energetic 18 months to three year olds, and give you a bit of relaxation and company.

Ask other mothers or your health visitor about groups in your area. Or look on the clinic notice board, or in newsagent's or toy shop windows. Your local library may also have information, and may itself run story sessions for pre-school children.

To begin with, your baby or toddler will want you, or another trusted adult, nearby for safety, but getting together with other parents will be good for you too. By the time your child is three, he or she will be ready to spend time without a parent or childminder to run to.

Playgroups, nursery schools, or nursery classes all have a lot to offer: more organised play of different kinds, the chance to be with other children and make friends, probably space to run around in.

Find out what's available in your area well in advance as there may be waiting lists.

PLAYGROUPS

Playgroups can be found in most areas. They vary in what they offer and how they're run. Some are free, others charge a small fee, though the amount varies. Sometimes you'll be able to leave your child, say for a couple of hours once or twice a week, so you can begin to get your child used to being away from you. Sometimes you'll be asked, or might want, to stay and help. Playgroups are often run by parents themselves.

"At playgroup he could run about and make a mess. At home there was just no room. He was happier and I was happier."

"I would worry about mine being looked after by someone else in case they didn't want to know me."

To find out about local playgroups
- Ask your Social Services Department (Social Work Department in Scotland; Health and Social Services Board in Northern Ireland) for a list of local playgroups.
- Contact the Pre-school Playgroups Association (address on page 133).
- You could join with other parents to start a playgroup yourself. The Pre-school Playgroups Association can help.

NURSERY CLASSES AND NURSERY SCHOOLS

A nursery class is part of an infant school. A nursery school is a separate school. Not every area has nursery schools or classes and in most areas they only provide sessions of about 2½ hours a day. A few will provide a full school day for four year olds. To find out what's available ask your education department (see page 123), your health visitor, other parents. Local authority nursery schools and classes are free.

INFANT SCHOOL

Legally children must start infant school no later than the beginning of the school term following their fifth birthday. Some schools take children earlier, but an early start isn't necessarily better, particularly if your child hasn't first been to a nursery class and had time to get used to being part of a large group.

Although parents are entitled to choose which school their child goes to, every school has a limit on the number of children it can take. So start looking at schools early, and check with the headteacher whether or not the school's likely to take your child. You can get a list of local schools from your education department (see page 123).

WHEN YOU CAN'T BE THERE

CHOOSING CHILDCARE WHILE YOU WORK

If you're returning to work you'll need to consider how your baby or child will be looked after when you're not there – not just the need for adults, but also for other children as companions.

Although playgroups and nursery classes rarely keep children for long enough to be useful to a working parent, they can still be used alongside other care from childminders or nannies, so they're worth keeping in mind as you consider your options.

All day care providers (with the exception of nannies who work in your home) should be registered with your local council social services department. Many councils provide handbooks for parents listing all the available care options.

For more on returning to work see page 120.

Childminders

A childminder is usually a mother herself and looks after a small number of children in her own home. Anybody paid to look after children under five in this way for more than two hours a day has to apply to register as a childminder with the local social services department. This doesn't apply to close relatives, but does apply to friends or neighbours. A childminder is usually registered to care for no more than three children under five, including any of her own. Registered childminders are visited by the social services to check that their homes are suitable and that they can give a good standard of care. So if you go to a childminder you don't know, it's worth asking if she's registered. You can ask to see her certificate.

You should be able to get the names of childminders with vacancies from your social services department. Other working mothers will also be able to tell you about childminders. If you don't already know mothers who use childminders, ask your health visitor to put you in touch.

Nannies, mother's helps, and au-pairs

Nannies, mother's helps and au-pairs don't have to be registered by the council, which means you don't have the safeguards which the registration of childminders provides. You can contact them through agencies, which will charge you a fee, or through advertisements in your local paper or national magazines. You could try advertising locally yourself.

If you employ a nanny you're responsible for paying her tax and national insurance as well as her wages. You may find that there's another working parent nearby who'd like to share the cost and services of your nanny. Parents at Work (see page 133) can provide you with more information on employing a nanny.

Au-pairs are young women or men who come from another country on a one year basis to learn English. If you invite an au-pair to live in your house he or she should not do more than 35 hours work a week. You provide bed and board and pocket money in return for child care.

Day nurseries

Day nurseries run by local authorities are quite rare. They often have long waiting lists, and only a limited number of places for very young children. Priority is usually given to parents who, for one reason or another, are under a lot of stress and are unable to cope, to parents of children with special needs, and sometimes to working single parents. To get a place at a council nursery, apply to your social services department. Your need will then be assessed by a social worker.

To contact your social services department, look in your phone book under the name of your local authority. (In Scotland the social services department is called the Social Work Department; in Northern Ireland it's the Health and Social Services Board.)

There may be nurseries in your area run privately or by a voluntary organisation. These nurseries must be registered with a local authority and you can find out about them through your local social services department.

You may be lucky enough to have a nursery or crèche where you work. If one doesn't exist, but there are a number of parents wanting and needing one, it's worth discussing the possibility with your employer. An organisation called Working For Childcare (address on page 133) can give you information.

Sharing/group care

Sharing/group care means getting together with other parents with needs like your own and organising your own childcare. This can work well if at least some of you work part time. Your health visitor may be able to put you in touch with other parents who work or want to work and need child care. The National Childcare Campaign (address on page 133) supplies information about setting up group care. If the group runs for more than two hours a day, and there is any payment involved, it will need to be registered by the local authority. Discuss what this will mean with the under-fives advisor at your local council.

THE COST OF CHILDCARE

The costs of childcare vary and can be very high. You'll have to ask. The cost of a nursery place may depend on your income. It's up to you to agree pay with a childminder, but your social services department may guide you. The National Childminding Association (address on page 133) also gives advice. In some areas, childminding fees are subsidised for low-income or single-parent families.

MAKING CHILDCARE WORK

- **First consider your child's needs and what is available.** There are few nursery places for babies and you may prefer leaving a small baby in the care of a single person who you can get to know. A toddler or pre-school child may be happier in a group atmosphere making friends and learning new skills,

 although a very shy child might prefer, for example, a childminder, but would like to be taken to a playgroup or one o'clock club to meet other children.
- **Your needs are important too.** Will the childcare cover your working hours or will you be looking for someone else to cover the extra time? If the arrangements are too complicated your child may feel anxious and you'll feel very stressed.
- **Before you decide on childcare, visit the childminder or nursery**, talk and ask all the questions on your mind (see the box on page 50 for ideas). Talk about hours, fees, what the fees cover, and what happens during holidays, when there's illness, or an emergency.

- **Consider transport arrangements.** How easily can you get there from work and from home?
- **It helps if children can settle in gradually.** If you can, start by leaving your child for short times and build up. This might mean starting to leave your child before you actually start your job.
- **Tell your childminder or nursery all about your child**, his or her routine, likes and dislikes, feeding information (particularly if you're still breastfeeding) and so on. When you leave or collect your child try to make time to talk and find out how things are going.
- **There may be special worries you want to talk about.** If your child has asthma, for example, you'll need to be sure that your childminder doesn't keep pets. You'll also want to know whether she, or any other people in the house, smoke. Or you may need to explain to a white childminder how to do a black child's hair. Perhaps you worry about your child being given certain things to eat. If this is important to you, it's right to talk about it. If childminders don't comply with reasonable requests their registration can be cancelled; consult your local under-fives adviser.
- **Make sure that you and your childminder or nursery workers can agree about issues such as discipline, potty training, and so on.**
- **Support and reassure your child in every way you can.** The early weeks are likely to be difficult for both of you. A regular routine, and a hand-over that's as smooth as possible, both help. Expect crying when you leave, maybe for longer than just the early weeks, but remember the crying usually stops once you've gone. You can ask how long it has gone on. It's best neither to linger long, nor to leave and then go back. Try to keep promises about when you'll return and explain to older children when that will be.
- **Chat with older children about the daily routine**, about the person or people caring for them, about what they've done while away from you. Try to show it's a part of normal life and something to look forward to.
- **It will help you to get into a routine**, and you need to make time with your child part of that routine. A lot of other things will have to go, especially the housework, but not sleep or meals. Share out the work at home with your partner if you can.
- **Children do well in high quality day care.** So you've no need to feel guilty about not always being there, but if you're worried about the quality of care then it's important to do something about it: talk to child carers, make an unannounced visit during the day, and if necessary, get details of any complaints procedure. Your child depends on you to keep him or her safe, secure, and happy.

"I wanted him to go to a childminder because I felt if I had to work that was a much more natural setting for him to grow up in... I don't know, though: maybe a nursery school would have been better where he could have learned to co-operate with people more."

"The first day was really terrible. I remember hoping that Andrew's salary would have doubled overnight and that I wouldn't have to go back. But now, I have to say, now I've got to know the childminder, I enjoy it. And even on the bad days when he's really crying I call the childminder and she says he's settled 10 minutes after I left."

Go to see the group or school

See a few if you have a choice. Talk to the people in charge, look at what's going on, ask questions (see box below).

Trust your feelings

If you like the feel of a place, and the children seem happy and busy, that's a good sign. You know best the kind of place that'll suit your child.

Talk to other parents whose children are at the group or school

Your health visitor may also be able to tell you about other parents' views and experiences.

Talk about ways of settling your child in happily

Staff may suggest ways of helping with this. At a playgroup or nursery school you might, for example, stay with your child at first, and then go away for longer and longer periods. Some children are helped by this sort of gentle start; for others a clean break seems to work best. Some take to change and separation quite easily; others find it hard. Be prepared to give support and reassurance for quite some time if needed.

In some situations, more support and reassurance may be needed. For example, it may be that your child will be one of very few black children at a mainly white school, or one of very few white children. In this situation, talk to the school beforehand about the kind of difficulties that a different colour, culture, or language might bring. Find out how the school will handle these, make suggestions yourself if you want to, and explain your child's needs. Talk with your child too, in whatever way seems best.

Questions you might want to ask

● How many children are there in a group/school/class, and how many staff?

● How many of the staff are permanent and what are their qualifications?

● What would your child's day be like?

● What sort of discipline is used?

● What facilities are there, such as equipment, space to play outside, space to run around inside when the weather is bad?

● Are trips and visits organised?

● What teaching is there about different races, cultures and religions?

● Are parents expected to help on a regular or occasional basis, perhaps with cooking or outings?

Habits and behaviour

4

There are some things that our children need to learn just so that we all get along together. The big issues for most parents are that our children should learn:

- to use a toilet
- to sleep through the night
- to behave reasonably well in public and private.

Sometimes we feel so anxious about these goals that we actually make it harder for our children to achieve them. This chapter helps you to step back a bit and see how you are managing.

POTTIES AND TOILETS

WHAT TO EXPECT

Children get bladder and bowel control when they're physically ready for it and want to be dry and clean. The time varies, so it's best not to compare your child with others.

- Most children can control their bowels before their bladders.
- By the age of two, one in two children are dry during the day.
- By the age of three, nine out of ten children are dry most days. Even then all children have the odd accident, especially when they're excited, or upset, or absorbed in doing something.
- At the age of three, two in three children are dry most nights.
- By the age of five most, but by no means all, children are dry at night.

LEARNING TO USE A POTTY
When to start

It helps to remember that you can't and shouldn't try to force your child to use a potty. In time he or she will want to use it. Your child will not want to go to school in nappies any more than you would want him or her to. In the meantime the best thing you can do is to encourage the behaviour you want.

"It's hard not to push them. You see these other children, you know, younger than yours, and they're all using the potty or the toilet, and there's yours, still in nappies. But they all learn in the end, and looking back, it wasn't that important. At the time, I thought it was dreadful because Al was the only child in nappies. But it was only me that minded. Al certainly didn't care, so what does it matter?"

Many parents seem to think about starting potty training around 18 to 24 months, but there's no particular time when success is guaranteed. It's probably easier to start in the summer, when washing dries better and there are fewer clothes, if any, to take off.

Try to work out when your child's ready. Most children go through three stages in developing bladder control:

- They become aware of having a wet or dirty nappy.
- They get to know when they are peeing, and may tell you they're doing it!
- They know when they need to pee, and may say so in advance.

You'll probably find that potty training is fastest if your child is at the last stage before you start. If you start earlier, be prepared for a lot of accidents as your child learns.

What to do

- **Leave the potty around where your child can see it and get to know what it's for.** If there are older children around he or she may see them using it and their example will be a great help. Let your child see you using the toilet and explain what you're doing.

- **If your child regularly opens his or her bowels at the same time each day, take off the nappy and suggest that he or she tries putting it in the potty.** If your child is the slightest bit upset by the idea just put the nappy back on and leave it a few more weeks before trying again.

- **As soon as you see that your child knows when he or she is going to pee, try the same thing.** If your child slips up, just mop it up and wait for next time. It usually takes a while for your child to get the hang of it and the worst thing you can do is make your child feel worried about the whole thing.

- **Your child will be delighted when he or she succeeds and a little praise from you'll make it better still**, but don't make a big deal of it and don't use sweets as a reward. You may end up causing more problems than you solve.

When the time's right, your child will *want* to use the potty.

PROBLEMS WITH TOILET TRAINING
Wet children

- **If your child shows no interest in using the potty, don't worry.** Remind yourself that in the end your child will want to be dry for him or herself. If your child starts to see the whole business as a battle of wills with you it'll be much harder.

- **Take the pressure off.** This might mean giving up the potty and going back to nappies for a while, or just living a wet life and not letting it get you or your child down. It might help to talk to someone about the best action. What you don't want to do is to confuse your child by stopping and starting too often.
- **Show your child that you're pleased and help your child to be pleased when he or she uses the potty or toilet or manages to stay dry, even for a short time.** Be gentle about accidents. You need to explain that it's not what's wanted. But do your best not to show irritation or to nag. Once a child becomes worried, the problem often gets worse.
- **Limit drinks a bit, and in particular cola or chocolate drinks. Many children go through a stage of demanding a lot to drink.** Try to make juice or milk 'special' rather than routine. Offer water in between. Most children drink less if it is only water that is offered. Some children drink for comfort or just for something to do. Offer other distractions, or another sort of comfort.
- **Many four to five year olds wet the bed.** It's often easiest to leave them in nappies at night. It saves washing sheets. You could try limiting drinks in the evening or getting your child up and putting him or her on the potty or toilet, say at the time you go to bed. Most aren't disturbed by this and settle again very quickly.
- **If your child has been dry for a while (night or day) and then starts wetting again, there may be an emotional reason such as a new baby or new house.** Be understanding and sympathetic. Your child will almost certainly be upset about the lapse and will not be doing it 'on purpose'.
- **By the time your child starts school he or she is likely to be just as upset by wetting as you are, so do all you can not to be angry.** Your child needs to know you're on his or her side and will help to solve what is now your child's problem more than yours.

Constipation and soiling

Your baby or child is constipated if he or she doesn't empty the bowel properly when going to the toilet (some stool stays inside). The stool is usually, but not always, hard and difficult to pass.

Another sign of constipation can be if pants are soiled with diarrhoea or very soft stools. This may happen because there is not enough fibre in your child's diet to keep things moving, or it can be something that starts as an emotional problem.

Most children simply grow out of wetting. If this does not seem to be happening when your child is ready for school, talk to your GP or health visitor about it. You may be referred to a clinic for expert help – not for your sake, but for your child's sake.

53

If your child continues to be constipated, talk to your health visitor or GP. If it's not sorted out in the end it'll become more of a problem for your child than for you, and he or she may need your helping in solving it.

Once a child is really constipated, even if passing a stool isn't painful they lose the sensation of wanting to go to the toilet, and it needs professional help to sort out.

- If your child becomes constipated, stools can become painful to pass out. The pain means that your child will then hold back even more, become more constipated, have more pain, and so on. It's important to stop this spiral. Ask your health visitor or GP to recommend a suitable laxative. If it doesn't solve the problem quickly, talk to your GP.

- Once the initial problem has been sorted out, it's important to stop it coming back. Make sure your child eats plenty of fibre. Fruit and vegetables, wholemeal bread, chapattis, wholegrain breakfast cereals, baked beans, frozen peas, and sweetcorn are good sources of fibre and children often like them. Also give lots to drink – clear drinks rather than milk. All this will help to prevent constipation.

- If dietary changes aren't helping, consider whether something could be upsetting your child. A young child may be afraid of using the potty. Be reassuring. Let your child be with you when you go to the toilet. And try to be as relaxed as you can be about it.

SLEEPING

In some families, children simply go to bed when they're ready, or at the same time as their parents. Some parents are happy to cuddle their children off to sleep every night. But others want bed time to be more organised and early enough to give their children a long sleep and them some child-free time.

Left to themselves most children will get as much sleep as they need. If it doesn't matter to you when that happens then you're unlikely to regard sleep as a problem.

If, however, your child's staying up late with you, but is then regularly woken early perhaps to go to a nursery or childminder, do be sure that he or she is having enough sleep. Your child may need an afternoon nap for longer than a child who regularly goes to sleep at 7.30 pm. Discuss this with your child's carers and make sure that they understand your child's individual needs.

When your child is ready to start school or nursery you may need to think again about late nights. It'll be hard to catch up on sleep in the day and it would be sad if your child was too tired to learn. You may find that bedtime naturally gets earlier as your child adjusts to a more demanding day. If not you may have to consider being a little more firm about bedtime.

REGULAR BEDTIMES

If you want your baby or toddler to get used to regular bedtimes, be clear, firm and consistent about what you want, and your child will gradually adapt.

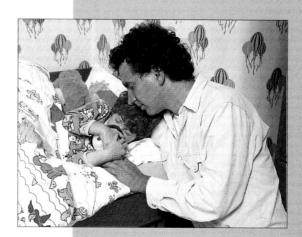

- **You stand a better chance of success if he or she is really tired, both mentally and physically.** Try to get outside at least once a day, and not just to give you exercise pushing the buggy. Get your child together with other children – they are good at tiring each other out. Find new activities. A change is often tiring, and something like going swimming can work the odd miracle.

- **Go through the same routine every night**, something like bath, games in the bath, story, quiet time to talk, sleep. Try to make it a time when you give time and attention, but wind down, and don't let the ending go on and on. Make it clear that at a certain point the day must and does come to an end.

CHILDREN WHO WON'T BE LEFT

If your child won't fall asleep without you then bedtime can become a trying and long drawn-out affair. Try getting your child used to falling asleep alone.

- **One week sit by the bed holding hands. The next sit further away. And so on.** Don't talk if you can avoid it.

- **Leave a light on.** Perhaps a ceiling or bedside light with a low bulb. Or try a dimmer switch. You can also buy glow plugs. They fit into an ordinary socket and give a very low light.

- **Try to get your child to go to sleep with a toy or some kind of comforter instead of you.**

- **Leave the radio or a tape on** (quietly).

- **Leave your child to play for a while if it helps.** Some children settle better if left to play for a while, perhaps in a slightly dimmed light. Others wind themselves up again this way, and then it's better to take toys out of the room, perhaps leaving one favourite quiet toy and a book.

- **If your child cries or makes a fuss when you leave the room, wait ten minutes, go back, resettle your child the same way as usual, and go away again.** Repeat this as often as you need or can bear, but be firm. You're saying 'I'm still here. I love you, but it's time for sleep.'

- **The important thing is *not* to give in.** If you've not been firm about bedtimes in the past then your child will expect you to let him or her get up. If this time you really intend to put a stop to late bedtimes then you must be clear. Give yourself time, try to be as relaxed about it as you can be, and make sure that your partner, or any other adults in the house, will support you.

- **Find out from your health visitor if there is a sleep clinic in your area.**

"When you've got the one, you don't know how easy it is. Once you've got the two of them, it's much more than twice the work. At the beginning, when the second's only a baby still, that's the most difficult time of all."

"When I only had one, if he had a tantrum, I found I could ignore it and stay fairly calm. Now, with the two of them, if I try to ignore anything, it turns into a full-scale war."

WAKING IN THE NIGHT

It's normal for babies and toddlers to wake in the night. Up to half of all children under five go through periods of night waking. Some will just go back to sleep on their own, others want company. The problem is not so much your child's waking, as your lack of sleep. There are two ways of coping.

Sleep with your child

Some parents like doing this anyway. If you have two children sharing one bedroom, and one is likely to wake the other, it can be the only answer. You may worry that it'll become a habit, and it's true that it may. But if it's a way of getting some sleep, that may be all that matters. It's possible to move some children back to their own beds once they've fallen asleep again and you may be able to teach your child to sleep alone when he or she is old enough to understand what you want.

Teach your child to fall back to sleep alone

- **First make sure that your child isn't waking from fear or bad dreams.** Try talking about it. Try and find the reasons – shadows? something seen on television? some family upset? – and sort them out if you can. Children don't normally wake from bad dreams much before two and a half to three years old.
- **If the reason isn't fear, then try to be firm and fairly brief.** Don't take your child out of the room. Don't start long conversations, stories, or games. Try to show that night-time is for sleeping, not company.
- **Make sure your child knows how to fall asleep without you.** If you cuddle or feed him or her to sleep every evening your child may be unable to get to sleep any other way. Look at the suggestions on page 55 and start by teaching your child to fall asleep alone.

A NEW BABY IN THE FAMILY

Coping with two children is very different from coping with one and it can be tough at first, especially if your first child isn't very old. So far as the baby goes, you've got more experience and probably more confidence, which helps. But the work more than doubles, and dividing your time and attention can be a strain.

It's not unusual for the birth of a second baby to alter your feelings towards your first child. It would be strange if it didn't. At first you may feel that you're somehow not loving your first one as much or enough.

Some parents say they feel very protective towards the baby and 'go off' the older one for a while. It simply takes time to adjust to being a bigger family and loving more than one child.

Your older child, no matter what his or her age, has to adjust too. You can probably help with this, and that'll help you.

- **Try to keep on as many of the old routines and activities as you can,** like going to play group, going to visit friends, telling a bedtime story. This may not be easy in the early weeks, but it gives reassurance.

- **Don't expect your older child to be pleased with the baby or feel the way you do.** It's lovely if the pleasure is shared, but best not to expect it.

- **Do expect an older child to be more demanding and to want more and need more of you.** Someone like a grandparent can often help by giving the older one time. But try to give some special attention yourself, and have some time alone together, so your older one doesn't feel pushed out.

- **Older ones don't always find babies very loveable, but they do often find them interesting.** You may be able to encourage this. There's a lot you can say and explain about babies, and children like to be given facts. Talk about what your older one was like and did as a baby. Get out the old toys and photos. And try to make looking after and playing with the baby a good game, without expecting too much.

- **Feeds are often difficult.** An older child may well feel left out and jealous. Find something for him or her to do, or make feeds a time for a story or a chat. With help, some older children can bottle feed a baby themselves.

- **Be prepared for your older child to go back to baby behaviour for a time** – wanting a bottle, wetting pants, wanting to be carried. It's hard, but don't always refuse requests, and try not to get angry.

- **There'll be jealousy and resentment, shown one way or another, sooner or later.** You can only do so much. If you and your partner, or you and a grandparent or friend, can sometimes give each other time alone with each child, you won't feel so constantly pulled in different directions.

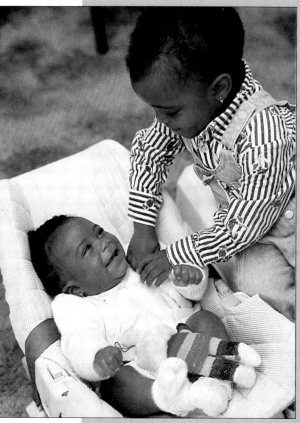

DEALING WITH DIFFICULT BEHAVIOUR

People have very different ideas about good and bad behaviour. What's bad behaviour to you may be accepted as normal by other parents, and vice versa. Sometimes it's a matter of a particular family's rules. Sometimes it's more to do with circumstances. It's much harder to put up with mess if you haven't got much space, or with noise if the walls are thin.

"I feel split in two. They pull me in different directions the whole time and it's almost impossible to do right by both of them. What's right for the baby is wrong for my older one, and the same the other way round. I love them both, but there doesn't seem any way of showing them that, or of being fair."

"You get a lot of advice about how to handle your children and I think, because a lot of the time you feel very unsure of yourself, you get to think there's a 'right' way. When you read something, or get a bit of advice, or see somebody handling their child a certain way, you forget to stop and think, you know, 'Is that me?'"

People react to their children's behaviour very differently. Some are tougher than others, some are more patient than others, and so on. It's not just a matter of how you decide to be. It's also how you are as a person.

It's best to set your own rules to fit the way you live and the way you are. And it's best to deal with your child's behaviour your way. But as for all parents there will be times when your child's behaviour gets you down or really worries you. There are times when nothing you do seems to work. What do you do then?

UNDERSTANDING DIFFICULT BEHAVIOUR

Try and step back and do some thinking.

Is it really a problem?

In other words, is your child's behaviour a problem that you feel you must do something about? Or might it be better to just live with it for a while? Sometimes it's trying to do something about a certain sort of behaviour that changes it from something that's irritating for you into a real problem for your child. But if a problem is causing you and your child distress, or upsetting family life, then you do need to do something about it.

It's also worth asking yourself whether your child's behaviour is a problem in your eyes, or only in other people's. Sometimes some kind of behaviour that you can happily ignore, or at any rate aren't worried about, is turned into a problem by other people's comments.

"The thing is that what you have to ask of them isn't always what you'd want to ask. It's how things are. My husband works nights and he has to sleep mornings. There's no way round that. If the children are noisy, he can't sleep."

Is there a reason for your child's difficult behaviour?

There usually is, and it's worth trying to work it out before you do anything. These are just some of the possible reasons for difficult behaviour.

● Any change in a child's life, like the birth of a new baby, moving house, a change of childminder, starting playgroup, or even a much smaller change, can be a big event. Sometimes children show the stress they're feeling by being difficult.

● If you're upset or there are problems in your family your children are likely to pick that up. They may then become difficult at just the time when you feel least able to cope. If a problem is more yours than your children's, don't blame yourself for that. But try not to blame your children either.

● You'll know your child's character and may be able to see that a certain sort of behaviour fits that character. For example, some children react to stress by being loud and noisy and wanting extra attention; others by withdrawing and hiding away.

● Sometimes your child may be reacting in a particular way because of the way you've handled a problem in the past.

For example, you may have given your child sweets to keep her quiet at the shops, so now she screams for sweets every time you go there.

- Could you be accidentally encouraging the behaviour you most dislike? If a tantrum brings attention (even angry attention), or night-time waking means company and a cuddle, then maybe your child has a good reason for behaving that way. You may need to try to give more attention at other times, and less attention to the problem.

- Think about the times when the bad behaviour happens. Is it, for example, when your child is tired, hungry, overexcited, frustrated, bored?

CHANGING YOUR CHILD'S BEHAVIOUR

Do what feels right

For your child, for you, and for the family. If you do anything you don't believe in, or anything you feel isn't right, it's far less likely to work. Children usually know when you don't really mean something.

Don't give up too quickly

Once you've decided to do something, give it a fair trial. Very few solutions work overnight. It's easier to stick at something if you've someone to support you. Get help from your partner, a friend, another parent, your health visitor, or GP. At the very least, it's good to have someone to talk to about progress, or lack of it.

Try to be consistent

Children need to know where they stand. If you react to your child's behaviour one way one day, a different way the next, it's confusing. It's also important that everyone close to your child deals with the problem in the same way.

Try not to overreact

This is very hard. When your child does something annoying not just once, but time after time, your own feelings of anger or frustration are bound to build up. But if you become very tense and wound up over a problem, you can end up taking your feelings out on your child. The whole situation can get out of control. You don't have to hide the way you feel. It would be inhuman not to show irritation and anger sometimes. But hard as it is, try to keep a sense of proportion. Once you've said what needs to be said and let your feelings out, try to leave it at that. Move on to other things that you can both enjoy or feel good about. And look for other ways of coping with your feelings (see page 60).

"Your children's behaviour takes over your life. I just felt that I changed totally when I had a second child. I felt my patience had gone completely. If I saw parents shouting in the street I used to think that was a terrible thing. When I had one, I could reason with her and we'd sort it out. When I had two, only one had to do something the slightest bit wrong and I would fly off the handle."

If you can think about your child's behaviour a bit and begin to understand it, you're more likely to find a right answer. And even if you can't find an answer, you'll probably cope better.

Talk

Children don't have to be able to talk back to understand. And understanding might help. So explain why, for example, you want your child to hold your hand while crossing the road, or get into the buggy when it's time to go home.

Be positive about the good things

When a child is being really difficult, it can come to dominate everything. That doesn't help anybody. What can help is to say (or show) when you feel good about something. Make a habit of often letting your child know when he or she is making you happy. You can do that just by giving attention, a smile, or a hug. There doesn't have to be a 'good' reason. Let your child know that you love him or her just for being themselves.

Rewards

Rewards can put pressure on a child, when maybe what's needed is to take the pressure off. If you promise a treat in advance, and your child doesn't manage to 'earn' it, it can cause a lot of disappointment and difficulty. Giving a reward after something has been achieved, rather than promising it beforehand, is less risky. And after all, a hug is a reward.

Smacking

Smacking may stop a child at that moment from doing whatever he or she is doing, but is unlikely to have a lasting effect. Children learn most by example. If you hit your child you're telling the child that hitting is reasonable behaviour. Children who're treated aggressively by their parents are more likely to be aggressive themselves and to take out their angry feelings on others who are smaller and weaker than they are. Parents do sometimes smack their children, but it is better to teach by example that hitting people is wrong.

WHEN EVERY DAY IS A BAD DAY

No parent 'does it well' all of the time. All parents have bad days, and most go through times when one bad day seems to follow another. Since you can't hand in your notice, or take a week off, you have to find some way of making life work.

When you're tired or in a bad mood, or when your child is tired or in a bad mood, it can be hard to get on together and get through the day. You can end up arguing non-stop. Even the smallest thing can make you angry. If you go out to work, it's especially disappointing if the short time you've got to spend with your child is spoilt by arguments.

Most children also go through patches of being difficult or awkward over certain things – dressing, or eating, or going to bed at night.

Knowing that it makes you cross or upset probably makes them still more difficult. And you become more and more tense, and less and less able to cope.

STOP! AND START AGAIN

When you're in a bad patch a change in routine, or a change in the way in which you're dealing with a problem, can be all that's needed to stop an endless cycle of difficult behaviour. Here are some ideas.

- **Do things at different times.** An argument that always happens at one time of day may not happen at another. And do the difficult things when your child is least tired or most co-operative. For example, try dressing your child after breakfast rather than before; have lunch earlier, or later. And so on.

- **Find things to do (however ordinary) that your child enjoys and do them together.** Let your child know that you're happy when he or she is happy. Every time he or she does something that pleases you, make sure you say so. We all prefer praise to blame and if you give your child lots of opportunities to see you smile the chances are that he or she will learn that a happy mother is more fun than a cross one.

- **Ask yourself whether the thing you're about to tell your child off about really matters.** Sometimes it does, sometimes it doesn't. Having arguments about certain things can get to be a habit.

- **When you lose your temper because you're tired or upset, say you're sorry.** It'll help you both feel better.

- **Don't expect too much.** You may think that sitting still and being quiet is good behaviour. Some children can manage this for a while. Others find it torture because they want to be learning and exploring every waking minute. If your child's a child who never keeps still and is 'into' everything, you'll be happier giving him, or her, as much opportunity as possible to run off steam and explore safely.

- **Don't expect a child under the age of three to understand *and* remember what they are allowed to do.** Even after the age of three it's hard for a child to remember instructions.

- **Don't expect perfect behaviour.** If you don't expect perfect behaviour then you won't feel so disappointed and angry if you don't get it. After all, if it's all right for you to be a less than perfect parent, then it's all right for your child to be less than perfect too. It's just hard to live with sometimes.

TALK ABOUT IT

It does help to talk and be with other people, especially other parents. It's often true that 'only parents understand'. A lot look very calm and capable from the outside (and you may too), but alone at home most get frustrated and angry at times.

"I've just stopped asking myself to be perfect. I've stopped trying so hard. You don't have to be perfect, and if you were, I don't think it would be that good for your child. People have to take me as they find me. That goes for the children, and it goes for people who drop in and find yesterday's washing-up in the sink and a heap of dirty washing on the floor."

"I think what's so wearing is that it all depends on mood. Not just their mood, but mine too. And you have to hide your feelings away so much, and they just let theirs out. If they want to lie down and cry because their favourite T-shirt's in the wash or you won't buy them something at the shops, they just do it. And when they do it in front of other people, that's awful."

You can talk in confidence to:
- **Parentline**
  01268 757077 (or in your local phone book)
- **NSPCC Help Line**
  0800 800 500
- **Parents Anonymous**
  0171 263 8918

"When it gets too much, I drop everything and get out. I go and see people, find somebody to talk to. I'm a different person when I'm with other people."

If you don't already know other parents living nearby, look on page 125 for how to find out about local groups. Groups don't suit everybody, but at the very least they're a way of making friends. And a group that is run by parents can often give more than friends who haven't got children the same age.

Sometimes it isn't your child whose mood is a problem. It's you. If you're miserable, trying to be happy for your child's sake may seem impossible. Read chapter 7 for more about this.

WHEN YOU CAN'T COPE

If every day is a bad day, and you feel that things are getting out of control, *get help.* Talk to your health visitor and/or phone a helpline (see page 61). Talking to someone who understands what you're going through may be the first – and biggest – step towards making things better.

Look on pages 133–6 for organisations that provide help and support to new mothers.

TEMPERS, TANTRUMS

Tantrums may start around 18 months, are common around two, and are much less common at four. One in five two year olds has a temper tantrum at least twice a day. One reason is that around this age children often want to express themselves more than they are able. They feel frustrated, and the frustration comes out as a tantrum. Once a child can talk more, tantrums often lessen.

- **Tantrums tend to happen when children are tired or hungry.** Sleep or food might be the answer.
- **If sleep or food isn't the answer, try to work out the reason and tackle that.** It may be frustration. It may be something like jealousy. More time and attention, and being extra loving, even when your child is not so loveable, can help.
- **Even if you can't be sure why your child has a temper tantrum, try to understand and accept the anger your child is feeling.** You probably feel the same way yourself very often. If you think about that, you may be better able to accept your child's feelings.

- **When a tantrum is starting, try to find instant distraction.** Find something to look at – out of the window, for example. Make yourself sound really surprised and interested in it.
- **If your child has a tantrum, try sitting it out.** Don't lose your temper or shout back. Ignore the looks you get from people around you. Stay as calm as you can, try not to get involved, but don't give in. If you've said 'no', don't change your mind and say 'yes' just to end the tantrum. If you do change your mind, your child will think that tantrums pay. For the same reason, don't buy your way out with sweets or treats. If you're at home, you could try walking away into another room.
- **Tantrums often seem to happen in shops.** This can be really embarrassing, and embarrassment makes it extra hard to cope and stay calm. Keep shopping trips short. You could start by going out to buy one or two things only, and then build up from there. Once you've managed one quick trip without trouble, you're beginning to make progress.
- **Some parents find it helps to hold their child, quite firmly, until the tantrum passes.** This usually only works when your child is more upset than angry, and when you yourself are feeling calm and able to talk gently and reassuringly.

HITTING, BITING, KICKING, FIGHTING

- **Don't hit, bite, or kick back.** It makes behaving like that seem all right. You can still make it clear that it hurts.
- **If you're with other children say you'll leave, or ask others to leave, if the behaviour continues – and do it!**
- **Talk.** Children often go through patches of insecurity or upset and let their feelings out by being aggressive – at play group, for example. If by talking you can find out what's worrying your child, you may be able to help.
- **Try to show your child how much you love him or her, even though you don't love the way he or she is behaving.** Children who are being aggressive aren't so easy to love. But extra love may be what's needed.
- **Help your child let his or her feelings out some other way.** Find a big space, like a park, and encourage your child to run and to shout. If there's nowhere to run, suggest that he or she shouts and punches a cushion, to get rid of the angry feeling inside. Just letting your child know that you recognise the feelings will make it easier for him or her to express them without hurting anyone else.

Help for difficult behaviour
You can get help for especially difficult behaviour, so don't feel that you have to go on coping alone. Talk to your health visitor or your GP, or contact your local child guidance clinic (you can sometimes go without a referral). Sometimes all you need is encouraging support to help you hold on until the problem is over.
Your child can also be referred to a specialist for help. If you've got a special problem, it's right to get special help.
Having a difficult child is an enormous strain. You need help too. Read page 112 for more on this.

OVERACTIVE CHILDREN

Many parents say their children are 'hyperactive'. In fact, real hyperactivity is rare, but quite a lot of children are extremely active, restless, and difficult to manage. And an overactive child, or even a 'normally' active child, will be much harder to handle if, for example, you live in a small flat.

- **Keep to a daily routine as much as you can.** Routine can be important if your child is restless or difficult. Routine may also help you stay calmer and stand up better to the strain.
- **Make giving your child time and attention a part of the routine.** In different ways, your child may be demanding your attention most of the day, if not most of the night as well. A lot of the time you'll have to say 'no'. This is easier to say, and may be easier for your child to accept, if there are certain times each day when you do give all your attention to your child.
- **Avoid difficult situations as much as you can – for example by keeping shopping trips short.** It's often no good even expecting an overactive difficult child to sit still at meals or behave well in a supermarket. And try lowering your expectations. Start by asking your child to be still, or controlled, or to concentrate, for very short times. Then gradually build up.
- **Try to get out every day you can to a place where your child can run around and really let go.** Go to a park, or a playground, or whatever safe, open space there is. Find ways of helping your child burn off energy.
- **Try cutting out cola drinks, tea and coffee.** These drinks all contain caffeine. Some children are sensitive to this and it can make them 'jumpy'. You can therefore try cutting them out and see if it helps.

Feeding the family

Food is one of life's greatest pleasures and yet it's also a source of worry for most parents. What should children eat? Can I afford to give it to them? Will they eat it? The next few pages will give you some basic guidelines on how to get your baby through the stage of weaning and on to family foods.

STARTING SOLID FOOD

WHEN TO START

For the first four months, babies can't properly digest any foods other than breast or formula milk. Other foods, in particular wheat (which is found in several baby cereals), may cause problems well into the future.

Most babies are ready to start solids when they are about four months old. (Premature babies should wait until four months past their *expected* date of birth. So if a baby is born 12 weeks early, he or she might be seven months old before starting solids.) Discuss this with your GP or health visitor. It's wise to introduce some solids by the time your baby is six months old, and gradually to build up so that solid food becomes the main part of the diet with breast or formula milk to drink alongside at least by the end of the first year.

GUIDELINES

All babies are different. Some start solid food earlier, some later. Some take to it quickly, some take longer, Some are choosy, others like anything and everything.

- **Go at your baby's pace.** Until now your baby has only known food that is a liquid and comes from a nipple or a teat. What you're doing is teaching your baby to take and enjoy food that has a different taste, a different feel, and comes in a different way. This is bound to take time.

"With your first baby, you worry about what you give them, and how much, and whether they'll like it. But with your second, it's much more like they have to fit in with the rest of the family, and you don't think about it so much. They take what's going, and they do it for themselves really."

"I think there's a lot of pressure on you to stop the breastfeeding and, you know, get on to something a bit more substantial. People are always sort of pushing you on to the next stage. It's hard to know what's best when people are saying to you 'Isn't she weaned yet?' and 'Have you tried this, have you tried that?'"

How can you tell when your baby is ready?
Your baby is ready to start solid food if he or she is between four and six months old and
● seems hungrier than usual
● starts to demand feeds more often
● starts waking again to be fed, after sleeping through the night.
If you've any doubts, talk to your health visitor.

● **In the end, you want your baby to be eating like the rest of the family.** So your baby needs to learn to like a variety of ordinary foods. In any case, variety early on might mean you avoid choosiness later. Your baby also needs to adapt to the family pattern of eating – say, three meals a day with a drink at each and two or three additional snacks – which will take time.

● **From the start, try not to rush and don't 'force feed'.** Most babies know when they've had enough to eat. Don't spend a lot of time persuading your baby to take food. Babies soon learn that refusing food is a good way of getting attention – or of getting a sugary pudding instead of a savoury first course! Of course it's right to give attention, chat, and enjoy meals together. But when food is refused, it might be best to call an end to the meal.

● **Once your baby starts to try and feed him or herself with fingers or a spoon, get ready for the mess.** Give one spoon to your baby while you spoon in most of the meal, and put newspaper on the floor. Babies do find their mouths sooner or later.

● **Cleanliness is important.** When preparing food for your baby, equipment should be really clean. Food standing at room temperature before or after preparation can be a breeding ground for germs. And it's not a good idea to store half-eaten foods.

● **Commercial baby foods can be useful, but don't let them replace fresh foods altogether.** Use mashed up family food when you can: it will get your baby used to eating what you eat. When you use commercial baby foods, follow the mixing instructions carefully and check that the seals on jars and cans haven't been broken. Look at the labels, first to check if the food is suitable for your baby's age and stage of weaning, second to check for unnecessary added sugars (see page 75 for more about sugar).

● **Always use a separate plate and spoon for your baby.**

STARTING SOLID FOOD

Step 1: the first two weeks of weaning

Start with a little vegetable or fruit purée with no added salt or sugar, or cereal (not wheat-based) on the tip of a clean teaspoon or your finger. Just a small teaspoonful is enough at first. Offer it to your baby after one of the milk feeds in the day, or in the middle of the feed if that works better. If you heat the food, make sure it's not too hot when you give it. If you use a microwave oven, be sure to stir well (parts of the food may be very hot even though other parts will be cool).

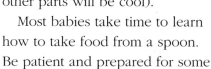

Most babies take time to learn how to take food from a spoon. Be patient and prepared for some spitting and mess. Your baby may also cry between mouthfuls at first. Until now, food has come in one continuous stream. Now there are frustrating pauses.

Don't press the food on your baby. If it really doesn't seem to be wanted, give up. Wait until next time.

Foods you might try

- Vegetable or fruit purées (potato, carrot, yam, plantain, spinach, apple, banana) ● Thin porridge (made from rice, cornmeal, sago, millet, for example) ● Baby rice and other first baby foods you can buy (use the instructions on the packet to make these up)

Don't yet give

- Wheat-based foods such as wheat cereals ● Milk other than breast or formula milk ● Eggs ● Citrus fruits ● Nuts ● Fatty foods ● Chillies or other strong spices

All can upset your baby or trigger an allergy (see 'Food allergic reactions' page 77).

Step 2: up to six months old

Feeds are still mainly breast or bottle, but now very gradually increase the amount of solid food you give either before, during, or after the milk feed. Try to follow your baby's appetite. Give the amount that seems to be wanted.

At the same time, move gradually from solid food at one feed in the day to solid food at two, and then three. Again, try to follow your baby's appetite and go at your baby's pace.

Try to keep cereals for one feed only. Begin to add different foods and different tastes. You'll be able to use lots of the foods you already cook for yourself.

Just mash, sieve, or purée a small amount (without added salt or sugar) and give it a try. Using your own family food is cheaper, you know what the ingredients are (halal meat, for example), and your baby will get used to eating like the rest of the family.

Foods you might now add

- Purées using meat (including liver) ● Poultry ● Fish ● Split pulses such as lentils ● A wider variety of vegetable and fruit purées

Still avoid

- Wheat-based foods (including bread) ● Milk other than breast or formula milk ● Eggs ● Citrus fruits ● Nuts ● Fatty foods ● Chillies and other strong spices

Do not use follow-on milk to replace breast or formula milk before six months.

Step 3: six to nine months old

Once your baby has grown used to a variety of foods, you can begin to give the solids first and the milk feed second.

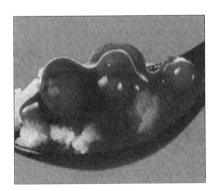

Your baby will gradually learn to cope with food that's lumpier. You can move on from purées to food that's just mashed with a fork or minced.

Stick with breast or formula milk for drinking in the first year. You can begin to use whole, pasteurised cow's milk after six months but only for mixing food. You can also move on to natural fruit juice (diluted at least five parts water to one part juice) or water as a drink with meals.

Foods you can now add

- Wheat-based foods ● Dairy foods (eg yoghurt and cottage cheese) ● Citrus fruits ● Well-cooked eggs ● Smooth peanut butter

In other words, you can now give almost any family food, provided you can make it the right consistency for your baby.

Step 4: from eight to nine months old

Once your baby can hold and handle things, try giving a piece of peeled apple, a scrubbed carrot, a crust of bread, or a bit of pitta bread or chapatti. This gives good chewing practice and it will help your baby to learn to feed himself or herself. Stay nearby in case of choking. Avoid things like sweet biscuits and rusks, so your baby doesn't get into the habit of expecting sweet snacks. Even low-sugar rusks contain sugar.

Continue to give breast or formula milk, rather than doorstep (cow's) milk. You can give follow-on milk if you like.

When your baby begins to chew, you'll only have to chop up food. Pieces of fruit, sandwiches and toast can become part of a day's menu. Look on page 71 for information on how to provide a good diet for your whole family.

Beware of these foods

● Don't add **salt** to your baby's food. A small baby's system can't cope with more salt than is naturally found in foods. When you're cooking for the family, leave out the salt so your baby can share the food. (It's better for all of you anyway without salt.)

● Adding extra **sugar** to your baby's food or drinks can give a taste for sweet things, which can lead to problems with tooth decay later (see page 31). If you use commercial baby foods go for the sugar-free varieties and encourage your baby to eat savoury foods as much as possible.

● **Wheat cereals, eggs, citrus fruits, nuts and peanut butter** may cause allergic reactions. Wait until your baby is at least six months old before you start giving them. Then introduce them in small quantities and one at a time, so you can watch for any reaction. Nuts should be finely ground to avoid the risk of choking. If anyone in your immediate family has allergies, it's possible your baby might too, so talk to your GP or health visitor first.

● **Eggs** should be thoroughly cooked until the white and yolk are solid. The white should be well mashed to avoid the possibility of choking.

● Use only **breast milk, formula** or **follow-on milk** in the first year. Give whole pasteurised milk as a drink at one year. If you are sure your child is a good eater, you can give semi-skimmed milk after two years.

● **Goat's and sheep's milk** should not be given before one year, and you should check that it is pasteurised or has been boiled.

● **Soya milks** can also cause allergic reactions. If a soya-based milk is recommended for your baby by a paediatrician or dietitian (instead of a cow's milk formula), you should use an infant formula soya-based milk. Don't use ordinary soya milk from a health food shop.

● **Nuts** shouldn't be given to babies and small children because of the risk of choking. Finely ground nuts and smooth peanut butter may be given after six months as long as there is no history of allergy in the family (see 'Food allergic reactions' page 77).

WEANING FROM THE BREAST OR BOTTLE

You can go on breastfeeding your baby alongside giving solid food for as long as you want to. If both you and your baby enjoy it, there's no reason to stop. A bedtime breastfeed can make a good end to the day.

Continuing breastfeeding or using infant formula (or follow-on milk after the first six months) during the first year ensures a good source of nutrients as well as being convenient and cheap.

If you use a bottle (or dinky feeder) don't put anything in it other than formula. Comfort sucking on sweetened drinks is the major cause of painful tooth decay in young children. It's a good idea anyway to wean from a bottle by the end of the first year as bottle sucking can become a habit that is hard to break.

It's a good idea to teach your baby to use a lidded feeding cup to give milk or cooled, boiled water any time after six months. Offer the breast or bottle as well at first, and gradually cut down. Or, if you think this puts your baby off the cup because there's something 'better' coming afterwards, try cutting out the breast- or bottle feed at one meal in the day and using the cup instead.

VITAMINS

You'll probably be advised to give your baby vitamin drops from the age of six months if breast milk is still your baby's main food. You'll be advised to give vitamin drops after 12 months if cow's milk is your child's main drink or if your child drinks less than 500mls of formula milk in one day. The drops contain the vitamins A, C, and D. Go on giving five drops a day until your child is at least two years old. By this age, many children are getting the vitamins they need from the food they eat and don't need extra. But if your child doesn't eat a wide range of foods, then it's probably best to go on with the drops until the age of five.

Vitamin D, which is important for strong bones, is different from other vitamins. It's found in some foods, but is also made by the body as a result of sunlight on bare skin. If you think your child may be short of vitamin D, especially during the winter months when children are indoors a lot, carry on giving vitamin drops until he or she is five.

You can get vitamin drops at most child health clinics. See 'Help with national health service costs' page 131 to check whether you can claim free vitamins.

ANAEMIA

Newborn babies have a store of iron that lasts about six months. Between six and 12 months it's important to prevent anaemia which can hold back their development. Babies can get iron from:

- a good mixed diet with meat and fish
- infant formula and follow-on milk (which have added iron) as their main drink.

If you are continuing breastfeeding and would prefer a vegetarian diet for your baby, ask your GP or health visitor about iron supplements.

FAMILY FOOD

MAKING THE MOST OF FOOD

Few of us have unlimited money and children who'll eat anything we put in front of them. We have to do the best we can with the money – and the children – we've got.

VARIETY

Variety's the first rule of good eating. Encourage your child to eat a wide variety of foods in the space of a day or a week: fruit and vegetables, as well as meat, fish, or pulses (peas, beans, lentils); dairy foods, as well as bread, chapattis, rice or pasta; and so on. If you provide a variety of foods, your child will almost certainly get all the nutrients he or she needs.

If your child's choosy, try to vary the menu as much as you can using the foods he or she will eat. It's usually possible to give even

---

Don't give any other vitamin supplements (such as cod liver oil) in addition to the drops. Too much of some vitamins is as harmful as not enough.

"Yes, I want my kids to eat the right sort of things. But wanting is one thing and doing it, or getting them to do it, is something else altogether. Mostly what one will eat the other won't. The only things I know they'll both eat are things like chips and sausages. Family meals almost always mean one of them making a fuss. You can make something for them that takes twice as long as sausages or whatever, and you end up putting it all in the bin."

"I've got 18 quid a week for the food and that's it. You don't get much choice for 18 quid. I know what I'd like to give the family to eat, and I know what I can afford to give them, and they're nothing like the same."

"When you go shopping, your mind's on anything but the shopping. You can't stop and think. You grab what you can and get out quick."

"It's difficult to give them healthy food because of the money. But some of the stuff that's not healthy costs most of all. Like sweets. And there are things you can do. Like beans and lentils and things are cheap and you can store them. And I slice up fruit and share it between the kids so it goes further."

"I do feel, you know, I wish she'd eat that. But I'm resigned to it, really. Because even getting her to try things is hard. So I just serve up the same old things, and it's a fairly good mix, so why worry? I mean, she does eat different sorts of food. She eats baked beans, she loves bread, she'll drink milk. Potatoes and cheese always go down OK. She has orange juice and apples, bananas sometimes. There's nothing wrong with that."

very choosy children some variety. You may find you go through stages of giving the same variety day after day, but this needn't matter. Gradually, over time, you'll be able to add new foods.

Set a good example yourself by sitting down and eating a meal with them. Mothers often neglect their own needs when caring for children, but you need to eat well to get the energy to care for them.

By about five years, children should be eating the sort of healthy diet that is recommended for the rest of the family.

Fruit and vegetables

Fresh, frozen, or tinned (but preferably not in brine or syrup) all vegetables contain vitamins, minerals, and fibre (which prevents constipation). Different vegetables and fruit contain different vitamins and minerals, so it's important to vary the kind, and particularly the colour. Try to include:

- some green vegetables
- some yellow or orange vegetables like carrots or swedes, or fruit such as peaches or apricots
- some citrus fruit or salad.

These will give your family a good range of vitamins and minerals.

Cook vegetables for just a short time in just a little water (or eat them in salads) to make the most of the vitamins. Many children won't eat cooked vegetables, but are happy to nibble on them while you're preparing them. You could mix vegetables together for variety – perhaps mashing or baking potatoes, carrots and courgettes together. Try giving fruit or bits of carrot instead of sweets between meals. If your child's fussy about eating vegetables and fruit go on giving vitamin drops. You can also give vitamin C enriched drinks with some meals for older children who no longer have milk as their main drink.

Iron

Iron is important in the diet for everyone, but particularly for women and children. The best way of ensuring that your whole family gets the iron they need is to offer small amounts of meat or fish every day. There's also iron in dark green vegetables, dried apricots, bread, nuts (but be careful – see page 69; nuts should only be given to babies over 6 months, and should be finely ground to avoid the risk of choking), beans and lentils, and in many infant and breakfast cereals. All these foods should be eaten with fruit, fruit juice, or vegetables (containing vitamin C which helps your body absorb iron). Breast, formula, and follow-on milks also provide good amounts of iron, but doorstep (cow's) milk is not a good source.

Starchy foods

Bread, chapatti, potatoes, pasta, rice and breakfast cereals (preferably without sugar, honey or added bran, which isn't suitable for young children) should, with vegetables or salads, form the main part of any meal. These foods are very important for the whole family because they provide the main source of energy as well as fibre and some vitamins. If your children are hungry fill them up on these foods. The wholegrain varieties (brown rice, wholemeal bread, or pasta) are particularly high in fibre, vitamins and minerals and can can be given as the children get older.

Meat, fish, eggs, poultry, beans, lentils (dhal), and nuts

These foods are the growth foods, rich in protein and minerals. Your child needs some of these foods at every main meal, but it doesn't have to be meat. Baked beans on toast provides plenty of protein, and so does a cheese sandwich (see page 74).

Healthy fast food
Fruit and vegetables
Wholemeal bread or toast
Baked beans
Baked potatoes
Fish fingers and frozen fish
generally, but grilled or
baked rather than fried
Tinned fish
Tinned tomatoes
Plain yoghurt
Cooked eggs
Wholegrain breakfast
cereals, which don't have to
be eaten at breakfast

"Everybody knows that sweets aren't good. But they love them. And the fact is, it's a pleasure to treat them."

"A lot of it is habit. I mean, if your children have never had sugar on their cereal in the morning, then they don't expect it. But then you mustn't have it either. The thing is that I like sweet things myself. In fact, at the moment, the more tired I get, the more I want to eat biscuits and that sort of thing. But if I eat them, the children eat them. The only answer is not to buy them in the first place."

Dairy foods (milk, cheese and yoghurt)

These are important foods for all the family. They provide protein for growth, vitamins and, most important of all, calcium, which is important for bones. During the first year breast, formula, or follow-on milks (after six months) should still be a major part of your child's diet. Later you can give whole pasteurised milk or other dairy products in different forms. Semi-skimmed milk can be introduced into the diet after two years if you're sure your child is a good eater. Skimmed milk isn't recommended for children under five years.

DRINKS

Milk (see above) will still be your baby's main drink for the first year. Carry on breastfeeding for as long as you and your baby want to. Cow's milk can be used as a drink after the first year (see above). When you start introducing other drinks, from about four months, stick to water or pure fruit juice (diluted at least five parts water to one of juice in the first year, and half and half after that).

Baby juices (including the new herbal drinks) are usually expensive and sweetened. Although they contain vitamins, it's better for babies and children to get vitamins from other sources.

Coffee, tea, cola drinks and many other children's drinks, contain caffeine, which may make your child irritable and hard to settle. Tea also contains chemicals that prevent iron from being absorbed from the food in the previous meal – and any added sugar is bad for the teeth. Bedtime drinks, such as hot chocolate and other sweetened milk-based drinks can be given, but only if you clean your child's teeth before he or she falls asleep. For the same reason, it's better not to give a bottle feed at night once children have teeth. Don't give your child fruit syrup and fizzy drinks.

SWEET TREATS

Children are born with a taste for sweet things. Breast and formula milk taste sweet and that's why they like them. It's tempting to go on giving them the sweet things that they like, but sadly, they're nearly always the things that do them no good.

Sweets, ice lollies, biscuits, cakes, fizzy drinks, and 'squash' are all produced to tempt the taste buds of children – and adults who have never grown out of their sweet tooth. Unfortunately they contribute to rotting teeth, fill us up, and spoil our appetite for the foods that do us good.

Giving a child sweet things may seem to be a nice thing to do, but in fact it just makes it harder for the child to learn to enjoy the taste of things that will be good for him or her. Nobody actually needs to eat, or add, sugar. There's already quite enough in the fruit and vegetables we eat.

That doesn't mean you should never, ever, give treats, but make sure they're treats – given on special occasions – not instead of good food.

● Give children unsweetened juices, diluted to reduce the sugar content, milk, or water, rather than squash and fizzy drinks.

● Cut down on cakes, biscuits, sweets, and chocolate in between meals as much as you can. There are lots of other things you can use for snacks.

Better snacks
Fresh fruit
Raw vegetables like carrots
Natural yoghurt with fresh fruit
Unsweetened breakfast cereals (with milk, or dry)
Bread
Unsweetened biscuits
Popping corn
Frozen peas

- Choose breakfast cereals that aren't coated in sugar or honey. They're usually cheaper. Don't sprinkle extra sugar on top.
- Read labels on tins and packets. Sugar may be labelled as glucose, sucrose, dextrose, fructose, maltose, or syrup. You can buy tinned fruit in natural juices rather than in syrup. Some tins and packets are now labelled as 'low in sugar' or 'without added sugar', but that may not mean much. If sugar is at the top, or near the top, of the list of ingredients then it's the biggest, or nearly the biggest, ingredient.

FATTY FOODS

Full-fat dairy products, fatty meats, fried foods, many convenience foods and cakes contain a lot of fat, and fat is very high in calories, which your body uses for energy. Children do need a lot of energy – and there are also some vitamins in fats – so some fat in the diet is necessary, but if your child gets more calories than he or she needs, there's a chance of becoming overweight. Good food habits start early and it's far better to cut down on fatty foods and fill your children up with bread, baked potatoes and pasta, rather than fried foods, cakes and pastry.

Try some of these ideas for cutting down fat in your family meals
- Grill or bake food instead of frying it. If you do fry, use an unsaturated oil like rapeseed, blended, vegetable, olive, soya, sunflower, or corn oil.
- Skim fat off fatty meat dishes, like mince or curry, during cooking.
- Choose poultry without the skin. The skin's the fattiest part.
- Trim the visible fat off red meat.
- Use vegetables or soaked dried beans with small amounts of meat in stews and casseroles.
- Use low-fat spread or a margarine high in unsaturates rather than butter, hard margarine, or ordinary soft margarine.
- Use lower-fat cheese like one of the low-fat Cheddars, Edam, or cottage cheese.

NOT MUCH SALT

It's possible to get all the salt your body needs from the salt that's naturally found in foods. So you really don't need to add salt to any food. For some adults, too much salt may lead to high blood pressure, and children who get the taste for salty food are likely to go on eating salt as adults. Cut down on salt as much as you can.

FOOD ADDITIVES

Any additives put into food must by law be shown on the label. Many are shown by the European Community E number. Additives with E numbers have been tested and passed as safe for use in EEC countries. Numbers without an E in front are allowed in the UK, but not in all EEC countries. Some additives are used to prevent food poisoning, or stop foods going off, but many are just flavourings or colourings.

Some additives are natural substances, some are synthetic. But the fact that an additive is natural, doesn't make it 'better'.

FOOD ALLERGIC REACTIONS

There are a few allergies to food which children do not outgrow and which may have a much more serious effect than other food sensitivities. An example is peanut allergy. For the majority of people, peanuts pose no problems.

However, in children who are allergic to them, a minute quantity of peanuts can lead to a life-threatening allergic reaction. The commonest symptoms in the very young are a sudden, sharp stomach pain, followed by swelling of the face, difficulty in breathing and shock. (The child will also look pale and have cold, clammy skin.) Similar symptoms may occur at any age, but the serious symptoms of this life-threatening allergy can occur without warning in older children.

Avoiding peanuts and peanut products is the best way to prevent a reaction in children known to be allergic, but since peanut oils are used in a variety of foodstuffs, this can be difficult. When a child has a reaction, immediate treatment is by an injection. Parents of children with diagnosed allergies to nuts can be provided with pre-loaded syringes to enable them to to give this treatment.

> **Parents who suspect their children may be susceptible to food allegic reaction should contact their GP, who can refer the child to a specialist clinic. The National Asthma Campaign Helpline (0345 010203) can also be contacted for advice.**

PROBLEMS WITH EATING

It can be a great worry if your child refuses to eat or is terribly choosy, but it is extremely rare for a child to actually starve him or herself. Children will eat enough to keep them going. So try not to worry unless your child is clearly not gaining weight as he or she should (see pages 34–5), or is obviously unwell.

It may be that your child is picking up your own feelings about food. Perhaps you're a dieter or have a weight problem, or maybe you just see healthy eating as a very important goal. If your child is picking up on your anxiety it maybe that mealtimes have become an ideal time to get attention.

Just as anxiety may cause problems with toilet training, it can also create problems with eating. So try and take a step back and think about how much of a problem there really is.

REFUSING TO EAT, OR EATING VERY LITTLE
- **Don't force your child to eat.**
- **Don't leave meals until your child is overtired or too hungry.**
- **If your child refuses food or just picks at his or hers for a long time, call an end to the meal.** Do it calmly and not in anger, no matter what time and effort you've put into the cooking.

- **Put less on your child's plate.**
- **Try to make meals enjoyable and not just about eating.** Sit down and chat about things other than food.
- **Sometimes a game to do with eating,** like lorries taking food to a depot, can help a child concentrate on eating. Sometimes games like this become the same as force feeding.
- **If you know other children of the same age who are good eaters, ask them to tea.** A good example sometimes works, so long as you don't go on about how good the other children are.
- **Ask another adult whom your child likes to eat with you.** Sometimes a child will eat for, say, a grandparent, without any fuss. It may be only one meal out of many, but it could break a habit.

- **If mealtimes matter then limit snacks and drinks between meals.**
- **If you don't mind much when your child eats, then provide snacks, but make sure they're not too sugary.**
- **Don't get trapped into giving your child a sweet treat after an uneaten meal.** It will give your child a very good excuse for refusing to eat and then holding out for the reward. You'll end up with a child who's living on sugars and fats rather than vegetables and bread.

BEING CHOOSY

- **Children's tastes change.** One day they'll hate something and a month later they'll love it. There'll nearly always be enough that your child is willing to eat for some variety (say beans, fish fingers, and fruit, and milk to drink). It may be boring, but it is perfectly healthy.
- **Carry on eating the variety of foods you like to eat.** It may seem easiest to cook only what your child will eat, but that's not going to be much of a diet for you, and your child will never get a chance to change his or her mind and try something else. Try to find meals where you can pick out one or two things your child will eat, and where you can eat the lot.
- **Let your child eat with other children, especially those who eat anything and everything.** Children who aren't very good about new foods will sometimes try them if they see other children eating them. Don't press – just let your child watch.
- **Don't get sucked into substituting sweet foods on the grounds that a cake is better than nothing at all.** A cake instead of fish fingers may be just what your child wants, but it's not going to help establish sensible eating patterns.

Illness and accidents

6

Every child gets ill occasionally and every parent has had that feeling of anxiety as they see their normally cheerful child looking sad and listless. Most bouts of illness pass quickly and leave children better able to resist the next attack. Sometimes, if the illness or accident is serious, immediate (and possibly long term) help is needed. This chapter deals with common childhood illnesses and accidents, the best ways to prevent them, and the action to take in an emergency.

KNOWING WHEN YOUR CHILD IS ILL

Sometimes there's no doubt. But often it's difficult to tell whether a child is ill. Children may be listless, hot and miserable one minute, and running around quite happily the next. Watch out for:

- **some sign of illness** (like vomiting or a temperature, cough, runny nose, runny eyes).
- **behaviour that's unusual for your child** (like a lot of crying, being very irritable or refusing food and drink, being listless or drowsy).

If you're seriously worried and/or know your child needs urgent attention, phone your GP at any time of the day or night. There may be a different number for when the surgery is closed. If you can't contact a GP, go directly to the nearest accident and emergency department. See inside the back cover for what to do in an emergency.

Possible signs of illness are always more worrying if your child is a baby or very small. For when to consult the doctor about your baby, see the box.

If your child is older and you're not sure whether or not to see the doctor, you might want to carry on normally for a while and see whether the signs of illness or pain continue. It might be best not to let your child see you watching. Most children can put on an act, especially if they see you're worried.

Above all, trust your feelings. You know better than anyone what your child is like day to day, so you'll know what's unusual or worrying. If you're worried, contact your doctor. Even if it turns out that nothing is wrong, that is exactly what you need to know.

If you have seen your GP or health visitor and your baby isn't getting better or is getting worse, contact your GP again the same day. If you become worried and you can't get hold of your GP or your GP can't come to you quickly enough, then take your baby straight to the accident and emergency department of the nearest hospital, if possible one with a children's ward. It's worth finding out in advance where this is, in case you ever need it.

USING YOUR GP

Most practices are very supportive towards parents of small children. Many will fit babies into surgeries without an appointment, or see them at the beginning of surgery hours. Many doctors will give advice over the phone. Others will feel that it's essential to see your child.

Some GPs are less helpful and it's not always easy to phone or to get to the surgery. Even so, if you're worried about a particular problem that won't go away, it's right to persist.

Your health visitor and/or clinic doctor can give you advice and help you decide whether your child is really unwell or not. But it's only your family doctor (your GP) who can treat your child and prescribe medicines. If you think your child is ill, it's best to see your GP.

If you're unsure whether to go to the surgery or ask for a home visit, phone and talk to the receptionist or to your GP. Explain how your child is and what's worrying you. Often it doesn't do a child (or anyone else) any harm to be taken to the surgery, and you're likely to get attention more quickly this way. But explain if it's difficult for you to get there. Wrapping a sick child up and going by car is one thing; going on the bus might be impossible.

USING MEDICINES

Medicine isn't always necessary when your child is ill. Some illnesses simply get better by themselves and make your child stronger and better able to resist similar illness in the future. If you're offered a prescription, talk with your GP about why it's needed, how it will help, and whether there are any alternatives.

- When a medicine is prescribed, ask about any possible side effects. Could it, for example, make your child sleepy or irritable?
- Make sure you know how much and how often to give a medicine. Write it down if need be. If in doubt, check with your pharmacist or GP.
- Always finish a prescribed course of medicine. A course of antibiotics, for example, usually lasts at least five days. This is to make sure all the bacteria are killed off. Your child may seem better after two or three days, but the illness is more likely to return if you don't finish all the medicine.
- If you think your child is reacting badly to a medicine, for example with a rash or diarrhoea, stop giving it and tell your GP. Keep a note of the medicine so you can tell your GP another time.
- If you buy medicines at the pharmacist, always say it's for a young child. Give your child's age. Some medicines are for adults only. Always follow the instructions on the label or ask the pharmacist if you're unsure.
- Always brush teeth after giving medicines. Ask for sugar-free medicines if they are available.
- Look for the date stamp. Don't use out-of-date medicines. Take them back to the pharmacy to be destroyed.
- Only give your child medicine given by your GP or pharmacist. Never use medicines prescribed for anyone else.
- Keep all medicines out of your child's reach and preferably out of sight – in the kitchen where you can keep an eye on them, rather than the bathroom.
- In the past, all medicines for children have been diluted to the right strength for each child with a liquid solution so that you could give it to your child on a 5 ml spoon. Now most medicines prescribed by your GP will no longer be diluted in this way. Instead you'll have to measure the correct dose for your child's age. The instructions will be on the bottle.
- Medicines that aren't diluted in liquid may need to be given using a 'liquid medicine measure', which looks like a syringe. It allows you to give small doses of medicine more accurately.

"He doesn't seem to listen. I'm in and out in no time, and I come home no better off than if I'd stayed at home. In fact, sometimes it makes it worse, because he'll give me something and I'll not know whether it's really needed or not."

"My doctor gives me advice. He's also a Moslem, you see, so he can give me advice about any questions I want to ask. He said if I had any worries, I could always go and talk to him."

Aspirin shouldn't be given to children under 12. It has now been linked with a rare but dangerous illness.

Paracetamol is safer, but don't give it to children under three months without asking your GP first. Make sure you've got the right strength for your child. Overdosing is dangerous. Read the label and/or check with your pharmacist.

Always read the manufacturer's instructions supplied with the measure, and always give the exact dose stated on the medicine bottle. Some medicines will come with a measure supplied by the manufacturer in which case that's the right measure to use. If in doubt ask the pharmacist for help.

LOOKING AFTER A SICK CHILD

It doesn't matter if your child doesn't want to stay in bed. Being with you, maybe tucked up in an armchair or on a sofa, might be less lonely. Children are usually sensible about being ill and if they say they're well enough to be out of bed, they very probably are.

- Keep the room your child is in warm (not hot) and airy.
- See page 86 for what to do if your child has a temperature.
- Give your child plenty to drink. For the first day or so don't bother about food unless it's wanted. After that, try to find ways of making a bit of food tempting.
- Try to give your child time for quiet games, stories, company, and comfort.
- Sick children are often easily tired and need lots of rest. Encourage your child to doze off when he or she needs to, perhaps with a story read by you or on tape.

Looking after a sick child, even for a couple of days, is exhausting. Make things as easy for yourself as you can. Get rest and sleep when you can, and try to get somebody else to take over every now and then to give you a break.

CHILDREN IN HOSPITAL

Hospitals can be strange, frightening places for children. Being ill or in pain is frightening too. There's no parent who isn't anxious to do all they can to help their child through.

- **Prepare your child as best you can.** You could play 'doctors and nurses' or 'operations' with teddies and dolls and read story books about being in hospital. It's worth doing this even if you don't know your child is going into hospital. Quite a large number of under-fives do have to go into hospital at some stage, and many go in as emergencies.

- **Be with your child in hospital as much as possible.** It's extremely important for you to be with your child in hospital as much as possible and, with young children especially, to sleep there. Do all you can to arrange this. All hospital children's departments now have some provision for parents to stay overnight with their children. Talk to hospital staff beforehand and be clear about arrangements, what will happen, and so on. You may then be able to explain at least a part of it to your child.

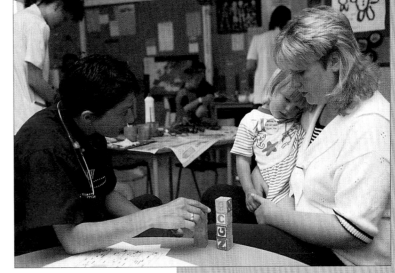

- **Explain as much as possible to your child.** Even quite young children need to know about what is happening to them, so explaining as much as possible is important. What children imagine is often worse than reality. Be truthful, too. Don't, for example, say something won't hurt when it will. Some hospitals will arrange visits for children and their families before the child is admitted for a planned treatment or operation.

- **Talk with hospital staff about anything that will be important for your child.** You may need to explain cultural differences. Staff should know, for example, if hospital food is going to seem very strange to your child. Try to discuss ways of getting over problems like this. Also tell staff about any special words your child uses (such as needing to go to the lavatory), any special ways of comforting, and so on.

- **Make sure something like a favourite teddy bear or comforter goes into hospital with your child.**

- **Be prepared for your child to be upset by the experience,** and maybe to show it in one way or another for some time afterwards. Reassure as much as you can.

You can get a lot of helpful information and advice on how best to cope when your child is in hospital from Action for Sick Children (address on page 134).

COMMON COMPLAINTS

Smoking and childhood illness

Children who live in a smoky atmosphere are more likely to get:
● coughs and colds
● chest infections (temperature with a bad cough)
● asthma
● ear infections and glue ear.

Every year 17,000 children are admitted to hospital because their parents smoke. If you can't stop smoking or encourage other adults in your house to stop, then try and make sure that your children don't have to smoke too by creating a smoke-free zone. See page 110 for tips on giving up.

Colds

● Children get so many colds because there are hundreds of different cold viruses. Young children are meeting each one of them for the first time. Gradually they build up some immunity and get fewer colds.
● Colds are caused by viruses, not bacteria, so antibiotics don't help.
● Sometimes babies who are snuffly can't breathe easily when feeding or asleep. Your GP may prescribe nose drops, which can help, or you could try gently tickling your baby's nostrils with some cotton wool – a sneeze might help to clear your baby's nose.
● A menthol rub or capsules containing a decongestant liquid, which you can put on to clothes, or a cloth, may help your child breathe more freely, especially at night. You can buy them from most pharmacists. You can also buy vaporizers, which can be helpful, but are expensive. Don't use menthol products for babies under three months without asking your GP, and be careful not to let your baby swallow a menthol capsule.

Colic
See page 20.

Constipation
See page 21 (babies) and page 53.

Coughs

● Most coughs, like colds, are caused by a virus, so antibiotics don't usually help. But if your child has a bad cough that won't go away, see your GP. If your child has a temperature and cough and/or is breathless, this may indicate an infection on the chest. If the cause is a bacteria and not a virus, your GP will prescribe antibiotics to treat this – although it won't soothe or stop the cough straightaway.
● If a cough continues for a long time, especially if it is more troublesome at night or is brought on by your child running about, it might be a sign of asthma. Some children with asthma also have a wheeze or some breathlessness. If your child has any of these symptoms, he or she should be seen by your GP. If your child seems to be having trouble breathing, contact your GP, even in the middle of the night.
● There is mixed opinion about the role of cough mixtures. In fact, coughing serves a purpose. When there is phlegm on the chest, or mucus from the nose runs down the back of the throat, coughing clears it away. If you want to soothe a cough, try a warm drink of lemon and honey, but there's no need to try to stop it completely.
● Croup is a result of infections which cause swelling at the back of the throat, along with difficulty in breathing. Your child will have a hoarse cough and noisy breathing. Contact your GP if you think your child has croup. Sometimes, though not often, croup can be life-threatening. Therefore, it is important to watch out for danger signals like:

● indrawing between the ribs or below the ribs with breathing
● restlessness
● irritability
● or blueness of the lips.
If you notice any of these signs, call your GP or, if a doctor is not available, take your child straight to the nearest hospital with an accident and emergency department.
● A steamy atmosphere helps to relieve a 'croupy' cough and ease breathing. If your child has an attack of croup sit with him or her in the bathroom with the hot tap running or in the kitchen with water boiling. But be careful: very hot water, even if it isn't boiling, can scald.

Diarrhoea
Young babies

Young babies' stools are naturally runny and yellow or orange coloured. But if you notice anything unusual about your baby's stools, they seem watery, and there are other signs of illness too, see your GP.

In the meantime, give your child plenty of fluid. Carry on breastfeeding, feeding more often if possible. Or, if you're bottle feeding, and the diarrhoea is constant, stop giving formula milk and give boiled cooled water, adding half a level teaspoon of sugar and a pinch (using two fingers and a thumb to make the pinch) of salt to every 8 fluid ounces/230 ml of water. Your GP can prescribe a rehydration mixture.

Diarrhoea in a baby can be dangerous, especially if he or she is being sick or has a fever as well, or if the weather is hot.

Older children

Contact your GP if your child is vomiting at the same time, or if the diarrhoea is particularly watery, has blood in it, or goes on for longer than two or three days. Otherwise diarrhoea isn't usually worrying – just give your child plenty of clear drinks to replace what's lost, but only give food if it's wanted.

Ear infections
● Ear infections are common in babies and small children. They often follow a cold and sometimes cause a bit of a temperature. Your child may pull or rub at an ear, but babies can't always tell where pain is coming from and may just cry and seem unwell and uncomfortable.
● If you suspect your child has an ear infection, take him or her to the GP. It's important, so go as soon as you can. Ear infections can cause hearing problems and need to be dealt with. Paracetamol may help lessen the pain in the meantime.

Fits or convulsions
Convulsions or 'fever fits' are not uncommon in children under the age of three, but can seem very alarming to parents. Although there are other reasons why children 'fit', fits are most commonly triggered by a high temperature. If you think your child is having a fit because of a high temperature it's important to cool them down immediately. See 'Temperatures' page 86 to find out how to bring a child's temperature down.

If your child has a fit
● If your child has a fit he or she may suddenly become rigid and staring. Sometimes the eyes will roll and the limbs start to twitch and jerk.
● Lie your child on his or her side or tummy to make sure he or she doesn't inhale vomit.
● Stay with your child to prevent injury. Wait for three minutes. Most fits will stop within three minutes. When it is over reassure your child, make him or her comfortable, and then call a doctor.
● If the fit hasn't stopped, dial 999, or get someone else to go

for help. Carry your child with you if there is no one to help you. If your GP isn't immediately available take your child to a hospital or call an ambulance. Stay with the child to prevent injury and move objects away from where the child is lying.
● Tell your GP that your child has had a fit.

Once your child reaches three years old it is unlikely that he or she will start having fits. If your child does start to have fits, they may stop as he or she gets older.

Head lice
Lots of children get head lice. It makes no difference whether their hair is clean or dirty. They catch them just by coming into contact with someone who's infested. When heads touch, the lice simply walk from one head to the other.

If your child has head lice
● An itchy scalp is often the first sign that your child has head lice. But by this time, the lice have probably been in the hair for several weeks. So check your child's hair after every wash for tiny white/grey eggs (or nits), which are laid close to the scalp, particularly behind the ears. Unlike dandruff, they're firmly attached to the hair and can't be shaken off.
● One untreated child can infect an entire nursery so do get treatment as soon as you discover it. Your health visitor or school nurse can advise you.
● You can buy a lotion from your pharmacy, which kills the lice and eggs. It's important to check with your health visitor or school nurse which one is being used in your area. The lotion is changed frequently, as the lice become resistant to it and it no longer works. If you cannot afford to buy the lotion your GP can give you a prescription. Follow the instructions carefully. The lotion kills the lice and nits, but the nits

don't wash off. You'll still be able to see some in the hair. It doesn't mean your child is still infected. If you want to get rid of the dead nits, you can use a special nit comb. You can buy one at a pharmacy.
● Check your whole family and treat them too if they've any evidence of having nits. Tell the parents of other children who play with your child. If your child attends a nursery or play group, you may not be able to get rid of head lice unless all the children in the nursery are inspected and, if necessary, treated at the same time. Notify the nursery or school so that the rest of the class can be inspected and treated as necessary.
● Brush and comb hair often. It helps prevent head lice taking hold.
● Frequent swimming will destroy any protective effects which the lotions may have.

Nappy rash
See page 22.

Sore throat
Many sore throats are caused by virus illnesses like colds or flu. Your child's throat may be dry and sore for a day or so before the cold starts.

Sometimes a sore throat is caused by tonsilitis. Your child may find it hard and painful to swallow, have a high temperature, and swollen glands at the front of the neck, high up under the jaw.

If your child has a sore throat and a high temperature, or is generally unwell, check with your GP. If the sore throat is caused by a virus, antibiotics won't be needed. But if a bacteria is the cause, antibiotics usually help.

Teething
See page 31.

Temperatures

Babies

Always contact your GP if your baby has other signs of illness (see box on page 80) as well as a raised temperature and/or if your baby's temperature is higher than 38.5°C (101° F).

If the doctor doesn't find a reason for the temperature, he or she will almost certainly want to send a urine specimen to the laboratory. A detailed test will show if your baby has a urine infection.

Older children

A little fever isn't usually a worry. Contact your GP if your child seems unusually ill, or has a high temperature which doesn't come down. It's important to encourage your child to drink as much fluid as possible. Cold, clear drinks are best. Even if your child isn't thirsty, try to get him or her to drink a little and often, to keep fluids up. Don't bother about food unless it's wanted.

Bringing a temperature down

This is important because a continuing high temperature can be very unpleasant and, in a small child, occasionally brings on a fit or convulsion (see page 85).

● Take off a layer of clothing or bedclothes.
● Try sponging your child's body, arms, and legs with tepid water. Don't dry the skin. As the water evaporates, it takes heat out of the body.
● Paracetamol (make sure it's the right strength for your child) will also help to lower the temperature.
● Give cool drinks.
● Don't wrap your child up.
● Make sure the room isn't too hot.

Worms (thread or white worms)

Many children get threadworms. You'll see them in your child's stools, looking like tiny white threads. Your child may have an itchy bottom and may scratch it a lot, especially at night.

If you think your child has worms, see your GP or ask your pharmacist for treatment. Everybody in the family has to be treated because the threadworm eggs spread very easily.

To prevent the infection spreading, make sure that everybody in the family washes their hands well and scrubs their nails before every meal and after going to the toilet.

Vomiting

Babies

Babies often sick up a bit of milk, some a lot, without distress. But if your baby is vomiting often or violently and/or there are other signs of illness, contact your GP straightaway.

Your baby can lose a dangerous amount of fluid if he or she is sick often, especially if your baby has diarrhoea as well. See under Diarrhoea for how to make sure your baby has enough fluid.

Older children

Older children can be sick once or twice without any bother and be well again quickly afterwards, or after a night's sleep. If your older child goes on vomiting, and/or there are other signs of illness, contact your GP.

Give your child plenty to drink – clear drinks rather than milk. Don't bother about food unless he or she wants it.

Taking your child's temperature

● Shake down the mercury in the thermometer.
● Hold your child on your knee and tuck the thermometer under his or her armpit.
● Hold your child's arm against his or her body, and leave the thermometer in place for at least five minutes. It may help to read a story or watch television while you do this. By the age of five your child may take a thermometer under his or her tongue, for about three minutes.

Normal body temperature

● Under the arm, normal temperature is slightly lower than under the tongue – about 36.4°C (97.4°F).
● Under the tongue, normal temperature is about 37°C (98.4°F), but may vary a bit.

Strip-type thermometers

Strip-type thermometers, which you hold on your child's forehead, are not an accurate way of taking temperatures. They show the skin and not the body temperature.

INFECTIOUS ILLNESSES

Immunisation can prevent, or lessen, the risk of catching many infectious illnesses (see page 90). The table on pages 88–9 gives details of the most common ones. You also need to know about hepatitis B and meningitis.

HEPATITIS B

Hepatitis means inflammation of the liver. This can be caused by the virus hepatitis B, which can be transmitted from an infected mother to her baby during pregnancy or at birth. A baby who gets hepatitis B so early will probably not be ill, but will usually become a carrier of the virus and may develop liver disease later in life. But, this is now preventable.

Nowadays, mothers-to-be are often screened for the virus using a simple blood test. Babies born to infected mothers are then started very soon after birth on a three-dose course of hepatitis B vaccine. This prevents them from becoming carriers or developing liver disease.

If you'd like to know more about hepatitis B virus or hepatitis B immunisation, your health visitor or GP will be happy to talk to you. It's OK for an infected mum to breastfeed, provided the baby has had the immunisation.

MENINGITIS

Meningitis is caused by bacteria or viruses that infect the membranes covering the brain. It's a rare, but serious disease, especially in babies and young children. Although early treatment often brings about a complete cure, meningitis can cause various sorts of permanent damage and disability. It can also kill. There are two main types:

- Bacterial meningitis is less common, more serious, and needs urgent treatment.
- Viral meningitis is more common, usually less serious, and can't be helped by antibiotics.

It is difficult to tell the difference between bacterial and viral meningitis without hospital tests.

Until the Hib immunisation (see page 90) was introduced, meningitis caused by a bacteria called *Haemophilus influenzae b* (Hib) used to be the most common form of bacterial meningitis in the under-fours, and was most dangerous to children under one year. The Hib germs are found in the noses and throats of people who are perfectly well. It isn't known why some people who carry the germs develop meningitis and some do not. Children are more likely to be affected than adults because they have less natural immunity. This form of meningitis is now rare in the UK because of immunisation.

Occasional outbreaks of one of the serious bacterial types, meningococcal meningitis, continue to make it a cause for concern. This form of meningitis is now rare in the UK.

Warning signs for meningitis

Remember that even if your child has been immunised against Hib he or she's not protected against other forms of meningitis.

Meningitis can develop very quickly. If your child has any of the following, particularly a rash of small red spots or bruises, make sure you get IMMEDIATE medical help. The following symptoms may not all appear at the same time; some may not appear at all.

Symptoms of meningitis

In babies

High temperature

Fretfulness or distress

Vomiting/Refusing feeds

High pitched, moaning cry

Difficult to wake

Pale or blotchy skin colour

In older children

Rash of red/purple spots or bruises anywhere on body

Headache/Fever

Neck stiffness

Joint pains

Drowsiness or confusion

Dislike of bright lights

What to do

If you're worried about your child, call your GP straightaway to get advice. It's important to recognise meningitis early. If you're still worried after getting advice, trust your instincts. Go straight to the nearest accident and emergency department. Early treatment is essential if it is bacterial meningitis.

ILLNESS	INCUBATION PERIOD (The time between catching an illness and becoming unwell)	INFECTIOUS PERIOD (When your child can give the illness to someone else)	
Chickenpox	14–16 days	From the day before the rash appears until all the spots are dry.	
Measles	7–12 days	From a few days before the rash appears until five days after it goes.	
Mumps	14–21 days	From a few days before becoming unwell until swelling goes down. Maybe 10 days in all.	
Rubella (German measles)	14–21 days	One week before and at least four days after the rash first appears.	
Whooping cough	7–14 days	From the first signs of the illness until about six weeks after coughing first starts. If an antibiotic is given, the infectious period is up to five days after taking it.	

HOW TO RECOGNISE IT	WHAT TO DO
Begins with feeling unwell, a rash and maybe a slight temperature. Spots are red and become fluid-filled blisters within a day or so. Appear first on the chest and back, then spread, and eventually dry into scabs, which drop off. Unless spots are badly infected, they don't usually leave a scar.	No need to see your GP unless you're unsure whether it's chickenpox, or your child is very unwell and/or distressed. Give plenty to drink. Paracetamol will help bring down a temperature. Baths, loose comfortable clothes, and calamine lotion can all ease the itchiness. You should also inform the school/nursery in case other children are at risk. Keep your child away from anyone who is, or who is trying to become, pregnant. If your child was with anyone pregnant just before he or she became unwell, let that woman know about the chickenpox (and tell her to see her doctor).
Begins like a bad cold and cough with sore, watery eyes. Child becomes gradually more unwell, with a temperature. Rash appears after third or fourth day. Spots are red and slightly raised; may be blotchy, but are not itchy. Begins behind the ears, and spreads to the face and neck and then the rest of the body. Children can become very unwell, with cough, and high temperature. The illness usually lasts about a week.	See your GP. If your child is unwell give him or her rest and plenty to drink. Warm drinks will ease the cough. Paracetamol will ease discomfort and lower the temperature. Vaseline around the lips protects the skin. Wash crustiness from eyelids with warm water.
At first, your child may be mildly unwell with a bit of fever, and may complain of pain around the ear or feel uncomfortable when chewing. Swelling then starts under the jaw up by the ear. Swelling often starts on one side, followed (though not always) by the other. Your child's face is back to normal size in about a week. It's rare for mumps to affect boys' testes (balls). This happens rather more often in adult men with mumps. For both boys and men, the risk of any permanent damage to the testes is very low.	Your child may not feel especially ill and may not want to be in bed. Baby or junior Paracetamol will ease pain in the swollen glands. Check correct dosage on pack. Give plenty to drink, but not fruit juices. They make the saliva flow, which can hurt. No need to see your GP unless your child has stomach ache and is being sick.
Can be difficult to diagnose with certainty. Starts like a mild cold. The rash appears in a day or two, first on the face, then spreading. Spots are flat. On a light skin, they are pale pink. Glands in the back of the neck may be swollen. Your child won't usually feel unwell. Give plenty to drink.	Keep your child away from anybody you know who's up to four months pregnant (or trying to get pregnant). If your child was with anyone pregnant before you knew about the illness, let her know. If an unimmunised pregnant woman catches German measles in the first four months of pregnancy, there is a risk of damage to her baby. **Any pregnant woman who has had contact with German measles should see her GP. He or she can check whether or not she is immune, and if not, whether there is any sign of her developing the illness.**
Begins like a cold and cough. The cough gradually gets worse. After about two weeks, coughing bouts start. These are exhausting and make it difficult to breathe. Your child may choke and vomit. Sometimes, but not always, there's a whooping noise as the child draws in breath after coughing. It takes some weeks before the coughing fits start to die down.	If your child has a cough that gets worse rather than better and starts to have longer fits of coughing more and more often, see your doctor. It's important for the sake of other children to know whether or not it's whooping cough. Talk to your GP about how best to look after your child and avoid contact with babies who are most at risk from serious complications.

IMMUNISATION – THE SAFEST WAY TO PROTECT YOUR CHILD

What's immunisation?

Immunisation is a way of protecting children against a range of childhood diseases using a vaccine.

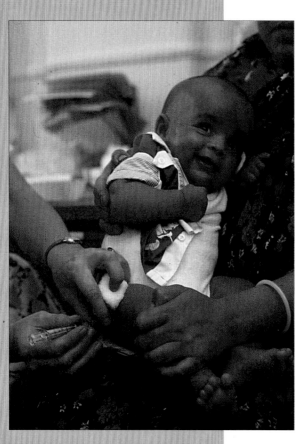

The injection, or medicine, gives the child a very tiny dose of the specially prepared bacteria or virus which causes the disease. As a result the child develops a natural defence system against any future attacks by that particular disease. The more children who are immunised, the rarer the diseases become. So immunisation protects not only your child, but young babies, other children, and adults as well.

Is immunisation effective?

Almost all children get long-lasting and effective protection from these diseases. However, no immunisation can guarantee complete protection. If a child does get the disease it's usually in a milder form. It's important to have the full course of immunisation to ensure maximum protection.

Does my baby have natural immunity to infectious diseases?

Very young babies have some natural immunity passed to them by their mother when in the womb, but this only lasts a short time, wearing off in two to three months for diphtheria, tetanus, whooping cough, polio, and Hib, and after about a year for measles, mumps and rubella. Breast milk contains antibodies, which help protect your baby against some infections. Formula milk used for bottle feeding doesn't contain these antibodies. Immunity to whooping cough can't be passed from mother to baby in breast milk. As whooping cough is particularly dangerous for young babies it's important for them to have their immunisations on time.

THE DISEASES

Many of these diseases are now rare, since most children have been immunised against them. But the diseases are still around and they can and do infect unprotected children.

Hib

Hib stands for *Haemophilus influenzae type b*. The main illnesses caused by this infection are meningitis (see page 87), epiglottitis (a swelling of the throat causing breathing problems), pneumonia, blood poisoning, and infections of the bones and joints. Before Hib immunisation was introduced, one in every 600 children caught Hib.

This resulted in around 65 deaths and 150 cases of brain damage each year in England.

Remember Hib immunisation only protects against one form of meningitis. You can read more about this in the leaflet *Protect your child with the new Hib immunisation* or, in Northern Ireland, *Protect your child – be wise, immunise.*

Whooping cough

Whooping cough is very infectious and can cause long, distressing bouts of coughing and choking up to 50 times a day for several weeks. It may also cause convulsions (fits), ear infections, pneumonia, bronchitis, collapsed lungs, sometimes brain damage, and even death.

Diphtheria

Diphtheria is rare, but serious. It begins with a simple sore throat, but quickly develops into a serious illness, which can last for weeks. It blocks the nose or throat, making babies choke and their breathing difficult.

Tetanus

Tetanus is caused by germs from soil, dirt, or dust getting into an open wound (especially a deep 'puncture' wound), or burn. It attacks the nervous system causing painful muscle spasms, which can affect the chest muscles and breathing. Because of immunisation it's now quite rare. Without immunisation, however, there's still a real chance of getting it because the germs are always present in the soil. It can be fatal.

Polio

Polio attacks the nervous system causing muscle paralysis, which can happen in any part of the body. When it affects the breathing muscles a child may have to be helped to breathe artificially and even then may die. If it affects the legs, they become weak or even paralysed – sometimes permanently. Polio has been eliminated in this country because of widespread immunisation, but could still recur. Many families travel abroad where there's a risk of coming into contact with polio, and, if they're unimmunised, bringing it back into this country. If you think you may not have been immunised yourself then speak to your GP and you can be immunised at the same time as your baby.

Measles

Measles is highly infectious and much more dangerous than most people realise. It always makes a child feel very unwell, but is also the childhood infection most likely to cause encephalitis (inflammation of the brain), sometimes resulting in brain damage. It can also cause convulsions and ear infections; and bronchitis and pneumonia, which can lead to long-term lung troubles. Measles can be fatal.

Going abroad
Your child may need extra immunisations. Check, at least two months in advance, with your GP or travel clinic (look in your telephone directory).

Mumps

Mumps is usually a mild illness, but can have serious complications. It's the most common cause of viral meningitis among the under-15s and can cause permanent deafness. Mumps can also be very uncomfortable for boys because it can cause painful swollen testes (balls). It can also cause a painful infection of the ovaries in women, so it makes sense to protect girls too.

Rubella

Rubella (German measles) is a mild disease, but if a pregnant woman who's not immune catches it, then her unborn baby can be damaged. The risk is especially high if it's caught in the first four months of pregnancy. The baby may then be born deaf, blind and with heart and brain damage. The most likely way for a mother to catch rubella is through contact with a small child (boy or girl) who has it, usually her own. So it's important for all children to be immunised. If you're uncertain whether you have yourself been immunised against rubella, speak to your GP.

Tuberculosis

Tuberculosis used to be a major killer, but today it can be treated and prevented. The disease may affect the lungs, brain (meningitis) and many other parts of the body. In some areas, teenagers are routinely tested for immunity and, if necessary, immunised at the age of 13. In some areas the BCG immunisation is also offered to small children. Your GP can explain the policy in your area.

THE IMMUNISATION TIMETABLE

The immunisation timetable (shown on the opposite page) is planned to give your child maximum protection as early as possible. The timetable is the same right across the country.

If your child has missed any of these immunisations, or started them late, don't worry. Your GP will tell you how to fit them in so that your child is fully protected.

YOUR CHILD'S IMMUNISATION RECORD

Tick the box and write the date each time you take your child to be immunised. Note any reactions in the space provided.

Time	Immunisation	Type	Date due	Date given	Reaction
At 2 months	Hib	One injection			
	Diphtheria ⎫ Whooping cough ⎬ DTP Tetanus ⎭	One injection			
	Polio	By mouth			
At 3 months	Hib	One injection			
	Diphtheria ⎫ Whooping cough ⎬ DTP Tetanus ⎭	One injection			
	Polio	By mouth			
At 4 months	Hib	One injection			
	Diphtheria ⎫ Whooping cough ⎬ DTP Tetanus ⎭	One injection			
	Polio	By mouth			
At 12–15 months (usually at 13 months)	Measles ⎫ Mumps ⎬ MMR Rubella ⎭	One injection			
3–5 years (around school entry)	Diphtheria Tetanus	Booster injection			
	Polio	By mouth			

REACTIONS AND SIDE EFFECTS

Your child may be unwell, irritable, or run a temperature. Contact your GP if you're worried, and especially if your child seems very unwell, has a temperature, becomes jittery, or screams continuously. If your baby is aged between two and three months, your GP will advise baby Paracetamol to help bring down any temperature (followed by another dose, if necessary, four to six hours later). Follow the dosage for your child's age given on the packet. If you're still not sure which dose to give, ask your GP. You can get a special oral syringe from the pharmacist for measuring the right amount.

DTP triple immunisation

Side effects from the triple vaccine (DTP) are almost always mild. Your baby may become fretful and slightly feverish within 24 hours of the injection.

Very rarely, a child may have a convulsion as a result of a fever after the immunisation. If this happens, the child usually recovers quickly with no lasting effects.

The whooping cough part of the triple vaccine is the one that some parents worry about most. Many people know how dangerous the disease can be, especially among the very youngest children, but remain unsure about whooping cough immunisation because of fears about the vaccine's safety. In fact, millions of children have been immunised against whooping cough without any evidence of harmful effects.

There has been a lot of research into the whooping cough vaccine but it has failed to find a convincing link between the *vaccine* and permanent brain damage. What we can say is that the chance of the whooping cough vaccine causing permanent brain damage is so small that we cannot count it. The risks of permanent brain damage from the *disease* are much greater.

Hib immunisation

About one in ten children may develop a small red swelling about the size of a milk bottle top after the Hib immunisation. This usually appears within three to four hours and disappears within 48 hours. The reaction, if any, will be less with each dose. Giving your baby the Hib immunisation at the same time as the DTP doesn't cause any greater reaction or side effects.

MMR immunisation

Most children are perfectly well after having the MMR (measles, mumps and rubella) vaccine. However, it's quite common for children to develop a mild fever and a rash, a week to ten days later, which should only last for two to three days. A few children get swollen faces or a mild form of mumps about three weeks after MMR. Any swelling will gradually go down.

None of these reactions are infectious. They're mild symptoms of the diseases themselves and do not usually need any treatment. Your health visitor or GP will be able to advise if you are worried.

Occasionally children do have a more serious reaction to the MMR vaccine. About one child in 1000 may have a febrile convulsion (see 'Fits' page 85), but a child is ten times more likely to have a 'fit' if they have the natural measles infection. Encephalitis (inflammation of the brain) following MMR immunisation affects less than one child in a million and most of these children make a complete recovery. In comparison, of those children who get the natural measles infection, about one in 5000 get encephalitis and one third of them will suffer brain damage.

WORRIED ABOUT THE COMPLICATIONS OF IMMUNISATION?

The risk of harmful complications from any of these vaccines is extremely small indeed. The risks of harmful effects from the diseases themselves are much more serious.

Some parents worry about possible harmful effects from immunisations, but vaccines have been given to many millions of children without any problems, and to enormous benefit.

You can discuss any worries you might have with your health visitor or GP, who will be able to advise you.

If your child is unwell on the day he or she is due to be immunised and has a fever, then discuss this with your GP or health visitor. There are very few genuine reasons why immunisations should not be done, but for your own peace of mind, talk to your GP in the following circumstances.

- If your child is unwell and has a fever. The injection will be delayed until your child is better.
- If your child has had a serious reaction to any previous immunisations.
- If your child has had a previous severe allergic reaction after eating egg. This means a swollen mouth and throat, difficulty in breathing, shock, or a general rash on the face and body, like the red and white patches after a nettle sting.
- If your child is taking medicines, particularly steroids.

HOMEOPATHIC REMEDIES

Some parents ask if homeopathic remedies are an effective alternative to normal immunisation. In fact there are no proven, safe, effective alternatives to immunisation. The Council of the Faculty of Homeopathy strongly supports the immunisation programme. They say that immunisation using conventional tested vaccines should be used as long as there are no medical reasons not to do so.

SAFETY

- Accidents are the commonest cause of death among children aged between one and five.
- Every year about 600,000 children under five go to hospital because of an accident in the home.

Children need to explore and to learn about the things around them. The safer you make your home, the less likely it is that their exploration will land them in hospital. Outside your home it's not so easy to make sure that the world is a safe place, but by getting together with other parents you can make a difference. You can put pressure on your local council as follows:

- to make road crossings safer
- to mend stairs and walkways and improve lighting
- to clear rubbish tips and board up old buildings.

PROTECT AND TEACH

- **Under-threes** can't be expected to understand or remember safety advice. They need to have an adult nearby at all times.
- **Three year olds** can start learning how to do things safely, but expect your child to forget if she or he is excited or distracted.
- **Eight year olds** can usually remember and act on safety instructions, though they are not yet safe enough to cross a busy road alone. They need adults around to call on for help at all times.
- **Under eleven years old** children are unable to judge speed and distance, so they should never cross busy roads alone. From the age of eight or nine children could cross quiet roads alone but they must wait until there are no cars at all. They should know and understand the green cross code.

SAFETY CHECKLIST

Use this list to check whether you're doing everything you can to prevent accidents. It's impossible to list all dangers, but thinking about some should start you thinking about others. Tick off the things you've done.

Danger – choking and suffocation

☐ Do you store small objects away from babies and small children who might put them in their mouths?

☐ Have you got rid of ribbons and strings that might, either in play or by accident, get wound around a child's neck?

☐ Do you keep peanuts away from children in your house? They often cause choking.

☐ Do you store polythene bags out of children's reach?

Danger – fires, burns, and scalds

☐ Have you fitted a smoke detector?

☐ Have you checked your smoke detector battery this week?

- ☐ Could you get out of your house in a fire?
- ☐ Have you shortened your kettle flex or bought a coiled flex? Dangling flexes from irons and kettles can be pulled.
- ☐ Do you have a fire guard, fixed to the wall, round any kind of open fire (coal, gas or electric) or a hot stove?
- ☐ Do you always use the back rings on the cooker and turn pan handles away from the front of a cooker? A flat work surface on either side of the cooker will prevent your child reaching pan handles at the side of the cooker.
- ☐ Do you use a playpen, cot or high chair (with restraints) to keep your child safe while you cook?
- ☐ Do you keep your child away when you're drinking or carrying hot drinks, and put mugs and cups, coffee jugs and teapots out of reach?
- ☐ Have you put your tablecloths away? A child pulling at the edges can bring a hot drink or teapot down.
- ☐ Do you always run the cold tap first in the bath and test the temperature before your child gets in? Be especially careful once your child is big enough to get into the bath without help and can play with the taps.
- ☐ Have you turned down the hot water thermostat to (54°C or 130° F) to avoid scalds?
- ☐ Do you always cover hot water bottles to prevent burns and remove them from the bed before your child gets in?

Danger – falls

- ☐ Do you always put bouncing chairs on the floor rather than a table or worktop?
- ☐ Do you have a properly fixed stair gate or barrier, preferably at both the top and bottom of your stairs?
- ☐ Baby walkers are dangerous. They tip babies down stairs, into fires, on to radiators. Don't tick this box until you have thrown yours out.
- ☐ Have you checked the rails round your landing and balconies? Could your child fall through, crawl under, climb over? Horizontal railings are especially dangerous.
- ☐ Do you have safety catches or locks on your upstairs windows to stop your child falling out? Are you sure you won't be locked or nailed in if there is a fire?

Danger – cuts

- ☐ Low-level glass in doors and windows is dangerous, especially once your child is on the move. Have you boarded it up, fitted safety film, or safety glass?

☐ Do you keep all sharp things somewhere safe (away from children)?

☐ Do you make sure your children never walk around holding anything made of glass or with anything like a pencil or lollipop stick in their mouths?

Danger – poisoning

☐ Have you locked all alcohol and medicines away or stored them high up, out of sight and where the child can't climb?

☐ Are your medicines in child-resistant containers? In other people's houses watch out for dangers like tablets in drawers and handbags.

☐ Are your household and garden chemicals in a safe place, high up, or locked away? Some chemicals are sold with child-resistant caps. Make sure you replace the cap properly after use.

☐ Are you sure there are no dangerous liquids in a bottle or jar that could make them look like drink?

☐ Are you teaching your children not to eat any plants, fungi, berries, or seeds?

☐ If you use surma on your child's eyes, is it one of the safe, lead-free brands? Talk to your pharmacist. Some surma can be dangerous.

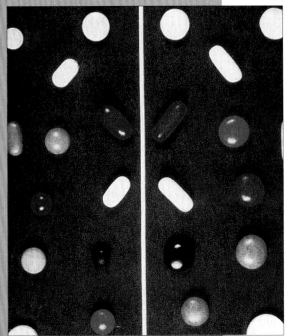

On the left are drugs, on the right are sweets

Danger – electricity

☐ Are your electric sockets covered by heavy furniture or safety covers when not in use?

☐ Have you repaired all worn flexes?

☐ Are you careful not to plug too many appliances into one socket?

Danger – drowning

☐ Do you know you should never leave a baby or young child under four alone in the bath for a moment? If the phone or doorbell rings, take your child with you, or let it ring.

☐ Is your garden pond covered or fenced off? Never leave your child alone near water.

☐ Does your child know how to swim? Children who can swim are safer, but it is still no guarantee of safety, so you should still keep a close watch when your children are near water.

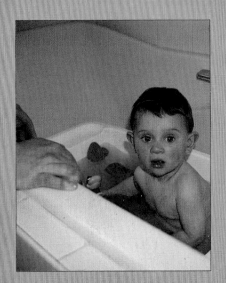

Danger – cars

☐ Do you know the law?

● It's illegal to carry an unrestrained child in the front seat.

● It's illegal to carry an unrestrained child if there is a suitable restraint in the car.

● If there's a child restraint in the front but not the back then children under three must use it.

● If there's an adult restraint in the front, but not the back children over three years must use it.

- You can only carry unrestrained passengers if there are more passengers than seat belts.

In general, it's safer for a child over three to use an adult belt than not to use a belt at all. Children should never be allowed to travel in the back of a hatchback (unless it has been specially adapted and fitted with seat belts) or to stand in a moving car.

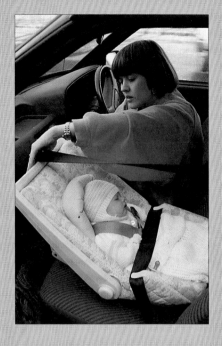

☐ Do you have a rear facing baby seat or a special restraint system for your carry cot?

☐ Do you have a child safety seat for toddlers?

☐ Do you have a booster cushion for bigger children to use with an adult safety belt?

☐ Do you always make sure you get your children out of the car on the pavement side?

☐ If you have air bags fitted to your car do you make sure your baby always travels in the back seat?

In a growing number of areas there are loan schemes for baby safety seats. Through these schemes, you can get the seats more cheaply. Some schemes are run by local maternity hospitals. Or ask your midwife, health visitor, or road safety officer.

Danger – roads

☐ Never let a child on or near roads alone. Young children don't understand the danger of traffic.

☐ Hold your child's hand when you're near roads. Walking reins are useful for toddlers.

☐ Teach your child to cross roads safely by always crossing safely yourself and explaining what you're doing. Don't expect any child under the age of eight to cross a road alone.

Danger – of strangers

Parents are often very worried about the possibility that their child will be abducted or murdered by a stranger. In fact this is a rare occurrence compared, for example, with the risk of a traffic accident. Nevertheless it's sensible to teach your children the following:

☐ Never go with anyone (even someone they know well) without telling the grown-up who is looking after them.

☐ If someone they don't know tries to take them away, it's OK to scream and kick.

Tell your children always to tell you if they've been approached by someone they don't know.

Make sure your child knows what to do if he or she is lost.

☐ In a crowded place, it's safest to stand still and wait to be found. Otherwise:

☐ tell a police officer

☐ go into a shop and tell someone behind the counter

☐ tell someone who has other children with them.

Teach your child his or her address and phone number or the phone number of some other responsible person.

EMERGENCY FIRST AID

In an emergency, try to keep calm. If your child is unconsious, follow the ABC of resuscitation shown on this and the opposite page.

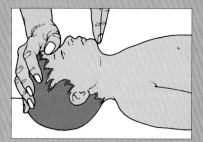

A OPEN THE AIRWAY
1 Place your child on a firm surface.
2 Look inside the mouth for any obvious obstruction which can be easily removed.
3 Put your hand on your child's forehead and gently lift the chin with two fingers.
DO NOT touch the back of the throat: young children's palates are very soft and may swell or bleed, further blocking the airway.

B CHECK BREATHING
1 Put your ear close to your child's mouth.
2 Look if the chest is rising and falling.
3 Listen for sounds of breathing.
4 Feel for breath on your cheek.
If your child is not breathing give five breaths of artificial ventilation (see page 101), then check circulation.

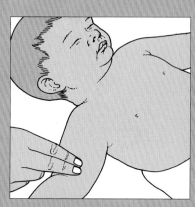

C CHECK CIRCULATION
For babies (under one year)
Check the pulse inside the upper arm by lightly pressing two fingers towards the bone.
For children (over one year)
Check the pulse in the neck by lightly pressing two fingers to one side of the windpipe.
If your child has a pulse but is not breathing
1 Start artificial ventilation (see page 101).
2 Continue for one minute, then carry your child to a phone and dial 999 for an ambulance.
3 Continue artificial ventilation. Check pulse every minute.
If there is no pulse after five seconds or if it is very slow (one beat per second)
Start chest compression (see page 101) together with artificial ventilation.
If your child has a pulse and is breathing
1 Place your child in the recovery position (see page 101).
2 Dial 999 for an ambulance.
3 Check breathing and pulse frequently.

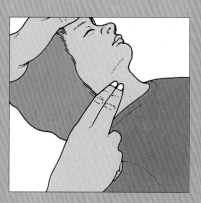

ARTIFICIAL VENTILATION

Babies (under one year)

1 Seal your lips around your baby's mouth and nose.
2 Blow gently, looking along the chest as you breathe. Fill your cheeks with air and use this amount each time.
3 As the chest rises, stop blowing and allow it to fall.
4 Do this at a rate of 20 breaths per minute.

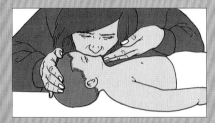

Children (over one year)

1 Seal your lips around your child's mouth while pinching the nose.
2 Blow gently, looking along the chest as you breathe. Take shallow breaths and do not empty your lungs completely.
3 As the chest rises, stop blowing and allow it to fall.
4 Do this at a rate of 20 breaths per minute.

RECOVERY POSITION

The aim of the recovery position is to keep the airway open and minimise further injury.

Babies (under one year)

1 Don't use the recovery position.
2 Hold your baby face down in your arms or your lap, in each case with the head held low.

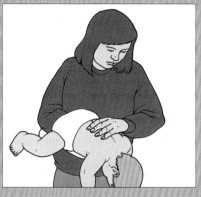

Children (over one year)

Note – for small toddlers it may be more practical to follow the guidelines for babies. Otherwise:

1 Place the arm nearest you at right–angles to the body, elbow bent. Bring the other arm across the chest. Hold the hand, palm out, against the cheek.
2 Roll your child on to his or her side, so that the upper leg is bent at the knee and the arms remain in the position described above.
3 Tilt the head back gently to maintain the open airway.
4 If in the correct position, as shown, your child will not roll on to his or her tummy or back.

CHEST COMPRESSION TOGETHER WITH ARTIFICIAL VENTILATION

Note – Chest compression must always be combined with artificial ventilation

Babies (under one year)

1 Place your baby on a firm surface.
2 Find the correct place to start the heart: a finger's width below the nipple line, in the middle of the chest.
3 Use two fingers and press down on the chest by 2cm (¾").
4 Press five times in about three seconds, then blow once gently into the lungs.
5 Continue this process for one minute.
6 Take your baby to a phone and dial 999.
7 Continue resuscitation (five presses followed by one breath) checking breathing and pulse every minute until help arrives.

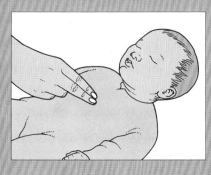

Children (over one year)

1 Place one hand two fingers' width above where the edge of the ribs meet the breastbone.
2 Use the heel of that hand and press down on the chest by 3cm (1¼")
3 Press five times in about three seconds, then blow once gently into the lungs.
4 Continue this process for one minute.
5 Take your child to a phone and dial 999.
6 Continue resuscitation (five presses followed by one breath) checking breathing and pulse every minute until help arrives.

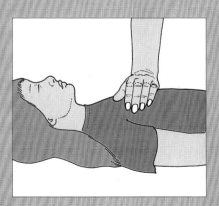

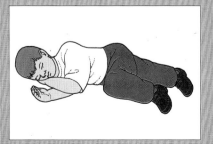

5 Check breathing and pulse. If either stops, follow the ABC of resuscitation.

101

IF YOUR CHILD HAS A BROKEN BONE...

- Don't move your child if you think his or her neck or spine may be injured. Get expert help. Unnecessary movement could cause paralysis.
- A bone in your child's leg or arm may be broken if he or she has pain and swelling, and the limb seems to be lying at a strange angle.
- If you can't easily move your child without causing pain, call an ambulance.
- If you have to move your child be very gentle. Use both hands above and below the injury to steady and support it (using blankets or clothing if necessary). Comfort your child and take him or her to hospital.

IF YOUR CHILD IS BURNT OR SCALDED...

- *Immediately* put the burn or scald under running cold water to reduce the heat in the skin. Do this for at least 10 minutes. If running water isn't possible, immerse the burn or scald in cold water or any other cooling fluid.
- Cover the burn or scald with a clean, non-fluffy cloth like a clean cotton pillow case or linen tea towel or cling film. This cuts down the danger of infection.
- If clothes are stuck to the skin, don't try to take them off.
- Call an ambulance or take your child to hospital. You should take your child to hospital for anything other than a very small burn or scald.
- Don't put butter, oil, or ointment on a burn or scald. It only has to be cleaned off again before treatment can be given.
- Don't prick any blisters. You'll delay healing and let in germs.

IF YOUR CHILD IS CHOKING...

Choking is caused by an obstruction in the airway and must be treated immediately.

- Look inside your child's mouth and remove any object if it is very easy to get at. Do not do this if there is any danger of touching the back of the throat as you could damage the soft palate.
- If your child isn't breathing, start artificial ventilation – it may be possible to ventilate your child if the obstruction is only partial. If your child is breathing, follow the instructions below:

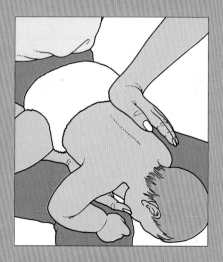

Babies (under one year)

1 Lie the baby along your forearm or thigh with the face down and the head low.
2 Give five firm slaps between the shoulder blades.
3 If this does not work, turn your baby on his or her back along your thigh head down. Give five chest thrusts using the same technique and finger position as for chest compressions (see page 101), but press more sharply at a rate of about 20 per minute.

4 If this does not work, dial 999 and continue repeating the sequence of back slaps and chest thrusts.

Children (over one year)

1 Encourage your child to cough if possible.
2 Bend your child forwards, so that his or her head is lower than the chest, and give five firm slaps between the shoulder blades.
3 If this does not work, lie the child on its back and give five chest thrusts.
4 If unsuccessful, give another five back slaps.
5 If this does not work, give abdominal thrusts. Place yourself behind your child and steady him or her with one arm. Put your other arm around your child, placing the heel of your hand in the upper abdomen. Give a sharp pull inwards and upwards below your child's ribs. Repeat up to five times.
6 If this does not work, summon medical aid and continue repeating the sequence of back slaps, chest thrusts, back slaps, abdominal thrusts.

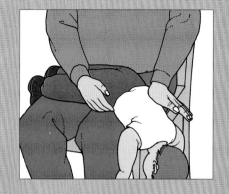

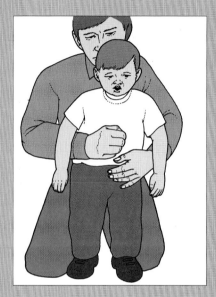

THINGS STUCK UP NOSE OR EARS...

If you suspect that your child has stuck something up into his or her ear or nose, don't attempt to remove it yourself (you may push it further in). Take your child to the nearest accident and emergency department. If the nose is blocked explain that he or she will have to breathe through the mouth.

IF YOUR CHILD HAS A CUT...

- If there's a lot of bleeding, press firmly on the wound using a pad of clean cloth. If you don't have a cloth, use your fingers. Keep pressing until the bleeding stops. This may take 10 minutes or more.
- Don't use a tourniquet or tie anything so tightly that it stops the circulation.
- If possible, raise the injured limb. This helps to stop the bleeding. *But don't do this if you think the limb is broken.*
- Cover the wound with a clean dressing if you can find one.
- Then call an ambulance or take your child to hospital.
- Ask your GP about a tetanus injection.

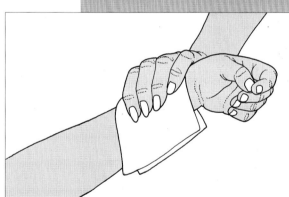

IF YOUR CHILD HAS TAKEN A POISON...

Pills and medicines

- If you're not sure whether your child has swallowed something, spend a minute or two looking for the missing pills. Check they haven't rolled under a chair, for example.
- If you still think something has been swallowed, take your child straight away to your GP or to hospital, whichever is quickest.

When to take your child to hospital after an accident
- **If your child is unconscious**
- **If your child is vomiting or drowsy**
- **If your child is bleeding from the ears**
- **If your child has stopped breathing at some stage**
- **If your child may have internal injuries**
- **If your child complains of severe pain anywhere**
- **If your child is having fits (see page 85).**

If you're worried or uncertain about your child's injuries, get a doctor's advice. If you are unsure of whether you should move your child, make him or her warm and call an amulance. Go to the accident and emergency department of your nearest hospital with a children's unit, or to a local doctor, whichever is quickest. Not all hospitals have an accident and emergency department, so check in advance where your nearest one is. Your health visitor will be able to tell you. (See inside the back cover for how to get help in an emergency.)

- If possible, take the container (or its label) with you and a sample of whatever you think your child has swallowed.
- Don't give salt and water to make your child sick. Large amounts of salt can be dangerous.

Household and garden chemicals

- If you think something poisonous has been swallowed, calm your child as much as you can. You'll do this better if you can keep calm yourself. But act quickly: get your child to hospital.
- If possible, take the container (or its label) with you and a sample of whatever you think has been swallowed.
- If your child is in pain, or there is any staining, soreness, or blistering around the mouth, then he or she has probably swallowed something corrosive. Let him or her sip milk or water to ease the burning in the lips. Get your child to hospital quickly.

IF YOUR CHILD IS SHOCKED...

- If pale, unwell, or feeling faint after an accident, help your child to lie down.
- If your child has lost a lot of blood, keep his or her head down and raise your child's legs. This makes more blood go to his or her head. But don't do this if you suspect a head injury or a broken leg.

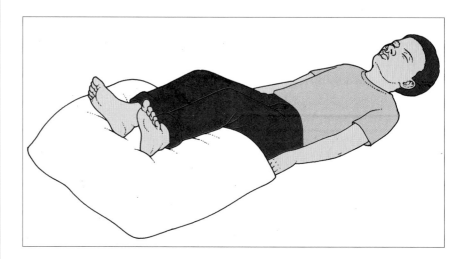

- Keep your child covered up and warm, but not too hot.

IF YOUR CHILD SUFFOCATES...

- Quickly take away whatever's causing the suffocation.
- If your child has stopped breathing, give artificial ventilation (see page 101).

WHEN A CHILD DIES

There's a feeling that children aren't meant to die. That feeling adds great shock (as well as maybe anger, bewilderment, even a kind of guilt) to the enormous grief and sadness brought by death. The grief, sadness, and other feelings are important to you. They're not to be set aside quickly or hidden away.

You need to let yourself grieve in your own way. If you need to cry, don't hold back the tears. Crying may be the only way of letting out your feelings. If you feel angry, as many parents do, or find you're blaming yourself or others, it's important to talk about it. Ask the questions you want to ask of, for example, hospital staff, your GP, midwife, or health visitor. Often the reasons for a baby's death are never known, not even after a post mortem. But you need to find out all you can.

After the first shock, it may help you to think about ways of remembering your child. If you don't already have photographs you may want to have a photograph taken to keep. Talk to the hospital about this. Give a lot of thought to any service or ceremony you may want, and to mementoes you may want to keep.

Try to explain what's happened as simply and honestly as you can to any older children. They need to understand why you're sad, and will have their own feelings to cope with. Sometimes an older child connects the death with something he or she has done, and may be very quiet, or badly behaved, for a time. It's not easy for you to give the love and reassurance that's needed. It may help to get support from others close to your child.

Coping with the outside world and other people is difficult at first. You may find that even people quite close to you don't know what to say, say the wrong thing, or avoid you. Take the support that's given and feels right.

It's best to expect a long time of difficult feelings and ups and downs. Talking may not come easily to you, but even some time after your baby's death, it can help to talk about your feelings. The more you and your partner can talk to each other, the more it'll help you both. A father's experience of a baby's death can be different from a mother's. Although you'll share a lot, your feelings and moods won't be the same all the time. Try to listen to each other so you can support each other as best you can.

Sometimes talking to someone outside the family is helpful – a close friend, your doctor, health visitor, hospital staff, maybe a priest or other religious counsellor.

"There was this huge emptiness, and the only way we could fill the emptiness and begin to understand was to talk and talk, and to cry. The real friends were the ones who let us talk and weren't afraid to see us cry. The last thing we wanted was to be helped to feel better. That would have meant forgetting what had happened to us before we'd even begun to live with it. It would have meant forgetting our baby. You never forget. It will always be part of us, just like any child."

"Time goes by and gradually, if you grieve enough, you begin to accept it. A time comes when you can make it all right with yourself to feel happy about happy things."

Talking to other parents who've been through the same loss and grief can be a special help. You can contact other parents through the following organisations.

● **The Stillbirth and Neonatal Death Society**
Run by and for parents whose baby has died either at birth or shortly afterwards.
● **The Foundation for the Study of Infant Deaths**
Supports parents bereaved by a cot death or what is called 'sudden infant death'.
● **The Compassionate Friends**
An organisation of, and for, all bereaved parents.

Addresses and phone numbers are given on page 135.

7

Your own life

Becoming a parent changes your life. Suddenly there seems to be no time for you; for the things you liked to do; for quiet moments with your partner or with friends. Sometimes you may feel that there isn't even any time for the basic things in life like eating and sleeping. But if you don't give yourself some time and consideration, your batteries will soon be used up and you simply won't have the energy to make a good job of being a parent. This section is for you.

"People say 'How's the baby doing?' And I want to say 'Well she's OK, but do you want to know how I'm feeling?'"

"I'm totally knackered, but I wouldn't give them back for anything!"

(A father) "I suppose I'd thought that having a kid wouldn't change that much for me. Obviously it was going to make a difference financially, with Linda giving up work. Apart from that, I'd thought it was Linda's life that was going to change and that I'd be going on much the same as before. Who was I kidding?"

YOUR BODY AFTER CHILDBIRTH

Having a baby changes your body. You may not like the changes, or you may enjoy feeling different 'more like a mother'. If you like the way you are, don't let other people tell you different.

If you feel uncomfortable with your body you'll want to make some changes. Some things will never be quite the same again – for example, stretch marks will fade, but won't ever go away completely.

Other changes need not be permanent. A saggy tummy can be tightened up with exercise, and weight gain will gradually drop off if you eat and exercise sensibly. But don't expect any of this to happen overnight. It took nine months to make a baby. Give yourself at least that long to get back into shape again – and it may take longer.

In the meantime, give your body some little treats to cheer you up. For example, if it makes you feel good to paint your toe nails, then make time to do it. Maybe for you that's even more important than 20 minutes extra sleep.

PHYSICAL PROBLEMS

A lot of women have physical problems, either as a result of labour and birth, or because of the kind of work involved in caring for young children, or both. Problems like some sort of infection that keeps coming back, back pain, a leaky bladder, and painful intercourse, are much more common than people think. These sorts of problems can get you down, and some get worse if they're not seen to.

I think everyone assumes that after the first month or so, you're back to normal again. But I know from talking to friends that I'm not the only one to feel like anything but normal."

"A frump. That's what I am. But where's the time to do anything about it?"

"I just don't like myself any more. My whole body's completely changed."

"You think you're the only person in the world with this problem, and you feel embarrassed and, you know, almost a bit ashamed, as though somehow it's your fault. So you just go on and try to forget about it or hope it will go away. And when it doesn't, you get really fed up. It was only because I got talking to a friend, and we found out we both felt the same, it was only then that I started to think, well, maybe I can do something about this. And because there were two of us, we had a bit more courage and could back each other up."

If you've a problem that is bothering you, don't ignore it – ask for help. Your doctor may be able to suggest treatment or might refer you to a specialist at the hospital or to an obstetric physiotherapist who can help with back and bladder problems and painful stitch scars.

HELPING YOURSELF

For some problems you can do a lot to help yourself. The muscles around your bladder, vagina, and back passage (the perineum) may be weak and that could be part of the reason for the 'falling out' feeling or leaky bladder that many women describe. Pelvic floor exercises can help. A bad back can also be helped by exercise, and by learning to use your back carefully.

Pelvic floor exercise

The muscles of the pelvic floor form a hammock underneath the pelvis to support the bladder, womb, and bowel. You use these muscles when you pass water, empty your bowels, and when you make love. Often they're stretched during pregnancy, labour, and birth. If you can improve their strength and function you're less likely to have a leaky bladder, and more likely to enjoy intercourse.

You can do this exercise either sitting or standing, when you're washing up, queuing in the supermarket, watching television – anywhere. You ought to do it for the rest of your life. It's an exercise that's just as important for older women as younger.

- Squeeze shut your back passage, close up and draw in your vagina, and close your front passage, all at the same time.
- Hold on for about five seconds, then let go.
- Do this no more than 10 to 20 times, but exercise several times during the day.

It helps to imagine you're stopping a bowel movement, holding in a tampon, stopping yourself passing water. In fact, the best way to find the muscles is to try stopping and starting (or slowing down) the flow of urine while you're on the toilet.

Curl ups

This exercise firms up your stomach and closes the gap in the abdominal muscles that opens up during pregnancy.

- Lie on the floor (rather than your bed) with your knees bent up high so your feet are flat on the floor.
- Pull your tummy in and gradually lift your head and shoulders, reaching for your knees with your hands. Then lower back down very slowly.
- Begin this exercise gently and build up.

To ease back problems

- While feeding, always sit with your back well supported and straight. Use a pillow or cushion behind your waist.

- Kneel or squat to do low level jobs like bathing your baby or picking things up off the floor. Avoid bending your back. Make your knees work instead. Change nappies on a waist-level surface or while kneeling on the floor.

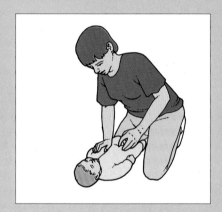

- To lift weights like a carrycot or an older child, bend your knees, keep your back straight, and hold the weight close to your body. Make your thigh muscles work as you lift.
- Try to keep a straight back when you push a pram or buggy or carry your baby in a sling.

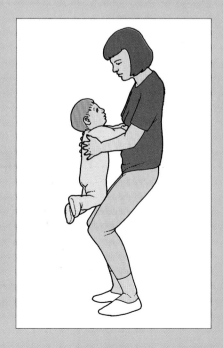

KEEPING HEALTHY

EATING

Eat well. Look back to **Feeding the family** page 65. If you can follow these guidelines, you'll be eating a healthy diet and be fitter and have more energy.

When there isn't time, or you feel too tired to cook much, try to find quick and easy food that is still nutritious. See page 73 for some ideas.

If you feel you need to lose weight, cut down on fat and sugar. Don't go on a crash diet. Small, regular meals will keep your energy levels up without adding to your weight.

"You get so used to managing without sleep and, you know, grabbing something to eat, it doesn't matter what, and just rushing on from one thing to the next. It's crazy really. I'll spend ages feeding the baby, but I don't feed myself properly at all. I'm anxious for her to sleep, but once she's off, I don't think about getting some sleep myself. Then I wonder why I'm feeling so rough..."

"You have to be quite tough with yourself. Because you tend to put things off. You say 'Oh well, I'll cook a proper meal tomorrow', or 'I'll start doing exercise again when I'm not so tired', or whatever. You get to think it doesn't matter and you just neglect yourself. I need my doctor to write me a prescription saying 'look after yourself'."

PHYSICAL ACTIVITY

When you're feeling tired, being more active or taking more exercise may seem like the last thing you need. But activity can relax you, help your body recover after childbirth, keep you fit, or improve your fitness, and makes you feel better.

- **Keep up the postnatal exercises you were taught.** Stick at them. They'll strengthen vital muscles and improve your shape. Some important exercises are described on page 108.

- **Join a postnatal exercise class if you've recently had a baby.** Company may help. Find out if your local maternity unit has a class run by an obstetric physiotherapist, or ask your health visitor about other local classes. If it isn't a special postnatal class be sure to tell the person running the class if you've had a baby in the last few months. You'll need to take special care of your back and avoid exercises that could damage it.

- **Push the pram or buggy briskly, remembering to keep your back straight.** Get out for walks as much as you can.

- **Play energetic games with older children.** Make yourself run about as well as them. Find outdoor space if there's no space at home.

- **Run upstairs.** You probably find yourself going up and down a hundred times a day in any case. Try to look on it as good exercise!

- **Squat down to pick things up from the floor holding heavy weights close to your body.** This is also something you're likely to be doing a lot. If you squat rather than stoop, bending your knees and keeping your back straight, you'll improve your thigh muscles. You'll also avoid damaging your back.
- **Join an exercise class.** There may be one locally that welcomes children or has a crèche. Ask your health visitor.
- **Swimming is good, relaxing exercise.** If you take your child with you, try to have someone else there too, so that you get a chance to swim.
- **Borrow or buy an exercise video.** Do a workout at home, perhaps with a friend. Get children to join in.

QUIT SMOKING

Many people smoke because they believe that smoking calms their nerves, but it doesn't. It just calms the craving for nicotine that cigarettes create. So here's how to stop.

- **Set a date.** Get rid of all your cigarettes, ashtrays, and lighters the night before.
- **Change your regular drink.** If tea and cigarettes always go together, perhaps you should try drinking something different.
- **Avoid smoky places.** Ask friends to meet you at home.
- **If your hands feel empty, try knitting.**
- **Take a walk.** If watching TV makes you want to smoke put on your coat and take a walk around the block.
- **Tell everyone around you what you're doing and why.** Ask them not to offer you cigarettes. If your partner or someone you live with smokes ask him or her to help you by stopping too.
- **Forever seems like a very long time so don't think about it.** Just stick with being a non smoker one day at a time.

Three good reasons to stop smoking
- Your children's health will improve.
- Your health will improve.
- You'll have money to spend on other things.

For help
Contact Quitline (see page 136). Their counsellors will give you help, advice or just encouragement. Their lines are open 24 hours a day and they can also give you details of your nearest quit smoking group. In Northern Ireland, contact the Ulster Cancer Foundation (see page 136). In Scotland, call the Smokeline (see page 136).

SLEEP

Most of the time parents just live with tiredness. But when the tiredness begins to make you feel low, bad-tempered, unable to cope, and certainly unable to enjoy things, you've got to find ways of getting more sleep – or at least more rest. Just one day, one night, one week, could help.

- **Get to bed early, really early, say for a week.** If you can't sleep when you get to bed, do something relaxing for half an hour beforehand, whether it's exercise, or soaking in a bath, or watching television.
- **Deep relaxation can refresh you after only five or ten minutes.** So it's worth learning a relaxation technique. You may find books, tapes, or videos about this at your library.
- **Sleep when your baby sleeps.** Rest when (if) your child has a daytime rest, or is at playgroup or nursery school. Arrange for a relative or friend to take your child for a while, not so that you can get the jobs done, but so you can sleep. Take turns with other parents to give yourself time to rest. Set an alarm if you're worried about sleeping too long.
- **If you can, share getting up in the night with your partner.** Take alternate nights or weeks. If you're on your own, a friend or relative may be prepared to have your children over night occasionally.
- **Look on page 16 for other ways of coping with disturbed nights.**
- **Do something about any stress.** Tiredness often comes from stress (see page 112). If you can do something about the stress, you may be able to cope better, even without more sleep.

"I think the tiredness is the worst thing. It goes on and on. And you've got no choice, you've got to keep going. So you feel sort of trapped. And after a bit, it gets you down, feeling so tired all the time."

(A father) "You come in from work and you start right in on another job. And then when you've got them off to bed, there are still other things you've got to do. So you drop into bed and there's been no breathing space. You're probably up in the night as well. And then you get up the next morning and start all over again."

"It's the two of them. What one wants the other doesn't want. When I'm getting the little one off to sleep, the older one suddenly decides he needs the potty. You can't seem to do right by both of them. You're split in two, and there's no let-up, it's the whole time."

"It's hard to explain to someone who isn't a parent how, even when you're enjoying it, there's this sort of constant drain on you. You think about them all the time, you have to. You have to think for them all the time. Even when I'm out at work, I have to think about getting back on time, and remembering to tell the childminder something, and buying something for tea..."

"It gets so frustrating. I wake up in the morning and think 'Right, what have I got today?' And then I give myself a great big long list of all the things I've got to do, and if I can't get them all done in that day, I get really narked about it."

COPING WITH STRESS

Small children ask a lot of you, and there's a limit to what you can ask of them. But perhaps the greatest stress comes from coping with the rest of life at the same time as coping with a baby or small child. You can spend a whole day trying to get one job done, but never managing to fit it in. Just as you start on it, your baby wakes up, or a nappy needs changing, or your child wants attention. Sometimes you can feel as though life is completely out of control. And if you're not the sort of person who can take things as they come and not mind about what is or isn't done, you can get to feel very tense and frustrated.

Stress also comes from worry and unhappiness: maybe to do with the place you live, money, relationships, or just a lot of small, but important things. You may not be able to change the way your children are or the life you lead. But you may be able to do something about the stress. It's a matter of finding solutions that are right for you.

● For you, relaxation may come from just doing something that you enjoy, can do for half an hour in the evening, and will put other things out of your mind for a while. A bath, maybe, or time to look at a magazine or the television. Do whatever will wind you down. Borrow a book or tape from the library about relaxation. Make yourself do it.

● See other people: it does take the pressure off. Try a mother and baby, or parent and toddler, group. Ask your health visitor or other parents about local groups. Or, if you're not keen on organised groups, get together with people you meet at the clinic, playgroup, or nursery school.

● Relationships can go wrong when you're tense and tired and never seem to see each other so make time to be with your partner, even if only to fall asleep together in front of the television.

- Talking about the stress you're feeling can help to get rid of it, at least for a while. If you and your partner can understand how each other is feeling, then take time to talk about how best to support each other. Sometimes it's better to talk with people outside the family (see below).
- Make the very most of all the help you can find. And give up a bit. You can't do everything. Try to believe it really doesn't matter.
- There are no prizes for being a supermum or superdad. Compromise if you're a perfectionist.

FEELING DEPRESSED

Most of us feel low occasionally and lack of sleep, stress, the strain of balancing paid work and parenting, and money problems, all contribute to making the early stages of parenthood a difficult, as well as a rewarding, time. Sometimes feeling low takes over completely and becomes depression.

Depression is more than feeling unhappy. It's feeling hopeless about yourself and all that's happening to you. The hopelessness can make you angry. But often you feel too tired even for anger. It can seem as though there's no answer and no end to the way you're feeling. You may feel all, or some, of these things:
- Tired, but can't sleep
- No appetite or are overeating
- No interest in yourself
- No interest in your baby
- The smallest chores are almost impossible to manage
- You never stop crying.

This kind of depression is like an illness. Nothing seems worth doing, so doing anything as demanding as caring for a baby or child becomes a real struggle. Both for yourself and for the family, it's important to get help.

See your GP or health visitor, or both. Take someone with you if this would help. Make it clear that you're not talking about just feeling low but something more worrying than that.

You may find that you're too low even to make the first step. If this is the case it's important to talk to someone: your partner, a friend, or your mother, and ask them to talk to your GP or health visitor on your behalf and arrange an appointment for you.

Talking it through

It does help to talk, but it may be very hard to do so.
- You may want to say things that you're afraid of admitting to the people you love.
- You may feel guilty about your feelings.
- You may believe that you'll be judged as a bad mother for admitting to them.

For all these reasons it's often best to talk to someone who isn't close to you, someone to whom you can be honest without being afraid of shocking them.

"They make me so angry. You wouldn't believe how wound up I get. Most of the time I sort of swallow it, but there are other times when they must hear me shouting down the other end of the block. I sometimes wonder whether other mothers get like that, because you see them walking down the street and they certainly don't look the way I feel."

Two organisations that offer help are the **Association for Post-Natal Illness** and **MAMA** (the Meet-a-Mum Association): their addresses are on page 133. Both organisations will put you in touch with other mothers who've been depressed themselves and know what it's like. Remember that what's called postnatal depression can happen a long time after the birth of a baby.

Alcohol may appear to help you relax and unwind. In fact it's a depressant, affecting judgement, self-control, and coordination. If you're tired and run down, it affects these even more. So watch how much and when you drink. Never mix alcohol with anti-depressants or tranquillisers.

"I think Dave thinks I've got an easy life, you know, just being at home all day. He thinks I can just suit myself and do what I want to do. I get very angry because there are days when I'd give anything to be walking out of the house like he does."

"There's a lot of pressure, it's true. I think we've had to learn a lot, and learn it fast, about how to get on when there's so much to cope with. But then there's a lot we both enjoy, and more to share, really."

You may find that it's enough to talk to your GP or health visitor, or they may be able to refer you to someone else. If you can talk about how you feel you'll almost certainly find that the things you fear are not as bad as you thought they were.

Medical treatment

If you're feeling totally lost in depression, your doctor may prescribe anti-depressant drugs. They may be enough to give you the lift you need to start coping again, and then to find a way out of your depression, though they can take time to work. Anti-depressants are *not* habit forming. You should not be concerned about them if they are prescribed for you by your GP. Tranquillisers may also be offered. They are different. They don't help depression and can be habit-forming so they're best avoided.

RELATIONSHIPS

PARTNERSHIPS UNDER STRAIN

Relationships are often strained by parenthood, no matter what they're like before. Part of the problem is that you have so much less time to spend with each other than you did before the baby arrived and it's so much harder to get out together and enjoy the things you used to do.

- Your partner may feel left out.
- You may feel resentful at what you see as lack of support.

The really hard time, when children take up all your energy, doesn't last for ever. Try and make time for each other when you can and do little things to make each other feel cared for and included.

"It felt like an invasion. All of a sudden, everything was revolving around the baby. For the first month or two I found it really hard. Now it's three of us and it couldn't ever be different, I couldn't imagine it back with just the two of us, but it was a very hard feeling, adjusting to the invasion of our privacy."

TIME TO LISTEN

Don't expect your partner, however close you were before the baby was born, to read your mind. Things are changing in both your lives and you have to talk about it. Your partner will not know what you want unless you say what it is and will not understand why you're resentful or angry unless you explain what's bothering you.

- Ask a friend or relation to babysit so that you can have time together – even if it's just for a walk together in the park.
- Share the housework to make more time just to be together.
- Share the babycare too.
- Talk about how you should bring up your children. You may find that you don't agree about basic matters about discipline and attitudes. Try to work out a way of working so that you're not always disagreeing in front of your children.

SEX

Babies and small children don't make for an easy sex life. Often you're tired, maybe too strained, and opportunities are limited. This hardly matters if both you and your partner are content. But if sex is a problem in any way at all, it's important to look at what you can do. Unhappy sex, or just lack of it, can cause a lot of frustration and worry, and can really strain relationships.

Immediately after the baby is born many women feel sore as well as tired. They may also be worried about the state of their body or about getting pregnant again.

Getting help
If this is your first baby you may be feeling very lonely and left out of your old life. Your partner can't supply everything that you used to get from work and friends. You need other people in your life too for support, friendship, and a shoulder to cry on. See 'Loneliness' page 120.
If you feel your relationship is in danger of breaking down, get help. **RELATE** (National Marriage Guidance) has local branches where you can talk to someone in confidence, either with your partner or alone. Counselling is offered on all sorts of relationship difficulties: you don't have to be married to contact marriage guidance. To find your local branch, look under **RELATE or Marriage Guidance** in your phone book, or write to the address on page 135.

Men can face problems too. Tiredness apart, a father's sexual feelings will probably be much the same as before his baby's birth. But many men worry about what's right for their partner, are unsure what to do, and feel worried and frustrated.

- **If penetration hurts, say so.** It's not pleasant to have sex if it causes you pain – and if you pretend everything is all right when it isn't you may well start seeing sex as a chore rather than a pleasure, which won't help either of you. You can still give each other pleasure without penetration.

- **Be careful the first few times.** Explore a bit with your own fingers first to reassure yourself that it won't hurt and use plenty of extra lubrication such as lubricating jelly: hormone changes after childbirth may mean that you don't lubricate as much as usual.

- **Make time to relax together.** There's little point trying to make love when your minds are on anything but each other.

- **Sort out contraception.** It's possible to become pregnant again soon after the birth of a baby, even if you're breastfeeding, and even if you haven't started your period again. So if you don't want to conceive again quickly, you need to use some kind of contraception from the start. Contraception is usually discussed before you leave hospital after your child's birth, and at the postnatal check-up. But you can go at any time, before or after a check-up, to your GP or family planning clinic, or talk with your health visitor.
- **If your baby sleeps in the same room as you,** you may have to move either yourselves or your baby before you can relax enough to have sex.
- **Don't rush. Take time.**
- **If you're still experiencing pain two months or so after the birth, talk to your doctor or family planning clinic about it.** Treatment is available for a painful episiotomy scar. Ask to see an obstetric physiotherapist.

LONE PARENTS

Bringing a baby into your life changes your relationships with other people whether you're part of a couple or alone with your child.

Some lone mothers feel that their own mothers are taking over, others resent the fact that their mothers won't help them more.

"The thing is everything's on your shoulders. When you have to decide something, you know, like whether or not to take him to the doctor, or even everyday small things, there's nobody to share that with. There are so many things it's useful to talk about, and if you're on your own, you can't. If there's a crisis, you're on your own."

"It's less stressful being your own boss. There's more satisfaction somehow, more achievement. There's no one to disagree with, no conflict over discipline, no competition with other adults."

"There's no company in the evenings. That's almost the hardest part. You put the kids to bed at night and that's it."

However painful it may be it's best to try and be very clear about the kind of help you do want, rather than going along with what's offered and then feeling resentful. Remember your mother's also having to get used to a completely new relationship with you and she won't know what to do for the best – unless you tell her!

You may find that your old friends stop coming by or that they seem to expect you just to drop everything and go out for the evening. Try not to get angry with them. They don't understand the changes you are going through. Keep in touch and keep some space for them in your life. Friends can be more valuable than money when the going gets tough.

You may be amazed and delighted at how much help you'll get from relations and friends if you ask! But the best support will probably come from other lone mothers.

● Suggest a 'swap' arrangement with another parent so that you take it in turns to look after both the children, by day to begin with, and later overnight. The children will benefit too from having a close friend, specially if they've no brothers and sisters.

● Suggest a regular evening babysit by a trusted relation or friend. You may well find that they're delighted at the opportunity of making friends with your child.

● Grannies are often glad to have a baby overnight, even if they don't much care for babysitting.

MAKING NEW FRIENDS

If you don't already know people locally try contacting other mothers through local groups.

● Ask your health visitor what's going on locally, and look through the list of support and information organisations on page 136. Many run local groups.

- **Gingerbread,** a self-help organisation run by and for one-parent families (address on page 135) has local groups around the country. Through these groups you can meet parents in similar situations to your own. And you can often help each other out as well as support each other generally.

MONEY AND HOUSING

Money may be a major headache. Look at **Rights and benefits** (pages 126–32) to check you're claiming all you're entitled to.

    The National Council for One Parent Families (address on page 136) offers free advice packs to lone parents and will provide independent advice about maintenance problems to women on benefits.

    If you need help with claiming maintenance contact the **Child Support Agency** helpline on 0345 133133 (local call charge). If you're on benefits your case will be handled automatically. If you're not on benefits, and want the agency to assess and collect maintenance on your behalf, there is a fee.

    See pages 123 and 130 for information about help with housing problems. If you are working, or thinking of it, see pages 46–50 for information about childcare.

ABSENT FATHERS

If you'd hoped to bring up your child as a couple you may be feeling very angry and hurt. One of the hardest things for a lone mother is to keep her hurt, angry feelings to herself and let her child make a different relationship with his or her father.

You'll almost certainly want (and need) to talk about your own feelings. Try to find another adult to talk to. Your children don't need to hear the details of your feelings about their father and will feel confused and unhappy about loving someone who you clearly do not love.

Unless your child's father is violent to you or the child, or you feel he's likely to abuse him or her in some way, it's almost certainly better for your child's own development if he or she is able to see his or her father regularly, even if you remarry.

You may find that your child behaves badly at first when he or she gets home. Small children aren't able to understand and explain how they're feeling and this is the only way they have of letting you know that they're confused. Unless you're convinced that something bad is happening on access visits, the best thing is to be reassuring and calm. In the end your child will learn to look forward to visits and also to coming home.

LONELINESS

Lots of mothers feel lonely. Especially after the birth of a first baby, many find that they're cut off from old friends, but it's difficult to make new ones. Getting out to see people, even if you've got people to see, is often an effort. Meeting new people takes confidence, but it's worth it. Having other people with whom to share the ups and downs of being a parent will help you to cope with the difficult times and make the good times better.

- Ask your health visitor for information about postnatal groups, mother and baby groups, parent and toddler groups, and playgroups. These may be advertised on the clinic notice board.
- Chat with other mothers at your baby or child health clinic.
- Talk to your health visitor and ask her if she could introduce you to other new mothers living nearby.
- MAMA, Home-Start, the National Childbirth Trust, and many other local organisations, sometimes based in a church or temple, run local groups where you can meet other people, chat, relax and get a lot of support. See 'Local groups' on page 125.

GOING BACK TO WORK

Most (or many) mothers go back to work at some point. About half do so before their children start school. It may help to talk to other working mothers. But also try to decide what's right for you and your family. (For information about childcare, see pages 46–50.) You'll need to think about the following.

- **Feeding.** If your baby is still breastfeeding, try to get him or her used to taking milk from a bottle or cup before you return to work. If you need help with combining work and feeding, discuss it with your health visitor, the National Childbirth Trust, La Leche League, or the Association for Breastfeeding Mothers (see pages 133–6). You can express milk to leave for feeds. It's also possible to give your baby formula milk in the middle of the day and still breastfeed the rest of the time.

"At first you hardly notice it. Your'e bound up with the baby, and there's such a lot to do. So you don't bother to meet up with people. Then you wake up one morning and you've got a whole day ahead of you and you know you're not going to see or talk to anybody, the whole day through."

Some mothers find the answer to feeling lonely and cut off is to take a job. It's not always easy to find the right sort of work with the right sort of hours, or to make childcare arrangements. But if you feel that work outside the home could help you, read the next section.

- **Childcare arrangements**. These must be as simple as possible to work smoothly. If they don't work smoothly, there's a lot of strain. You also have to be reasonably sure they'll go on working over time.
- **Paying for childcare.** Can you afford to pay for childcare out of what you earn? Can you find work that you can do while your partner is at home? Can you fit work into school hours? Can a relation help out? Is there any subsidised childcare in your area? (See page 48.)
- **Housework.** When and who'll do it? If you've a partner you need to talk about how you'll divide responsibilities for housework and childcare.
- **Making time for your child.** Even the best childcare isn't a substitute for a parent. Children need to know that they're special. If you work long hours during the week, can you or your partner keep your weekends completely free? If you don't see your child in the day, can you keep him or her up late in the evening and compensate with long day time sleeps? You may be able to work flexitime, part time, or a four-day week, and make a special time to be with your child.

"At first I hated leaving her. It was much more upsetting than I'd thought – but more for me than for her, really. I'm better about it now, especially as time goes by and I can see that she's happy and well looked after and I've got to know and like the person who cares for her. But I don't think you can ever feel completely right about it. So you just have to live with that and get on with it."

"There's no doubt it's hard work. I mean, there's no evenings off, because it's then that we have to get all the jobs done round the house. To my mind, families where there's one parent at home all the time have it very easy in comparison."

"I enjoy the job. It's nothing much, but it earns money we need, and it gets me out and makes me do things I'd not do otherwise. I think I'm a better parent for doing it. I like having contact with people other than mothers. And Darren gets to meet other children, and he thrives on that."

Your services

8

There are a wide range of services available from statutory organisations, voluntary organisations, and local groups. This chapter will help you find what you need. (Additional information for those living in Scotland and Northern Ireland can be found on p.123.)

HEALTH SERVICES

COMMUNITY MIDWIVES

Your community midwife has a legal duty to care for you and your baby for the first ten days after your baby's birth and will keep you on her books for the first 28 days if you, or the baby, need her. She can help with any problem to do with you or your baby and will give you a phone number to call at any time, day or night, if you need to.

HEALTH VISITORS

Your health visitor usually makes her first visit some time after your baby is ten days old. After that she may only see you at clinics or when you ask to see her. If you're alone, or struggling, she may make a point of coming by to see whether you need any help.

A health visitor is a qualified nurse who has had extra training to become a health visitor. Part of her role is to help families, especially families with babies and young children, avoid illness and keep healthy.

Talk to your health visitor if you feel anxious, depressed,or worried about your children. She may be able to offer advice and suggest where to find help, and may organise groups where you

can meet other mothers.

Your health visitor can visit you at home, or you can see her at your child health clinic, doctor's surgery or health centre, depending on where she's based. She'll give you a phone number to get in touch if you need to.

FAMILY DOCTORS

Your family doctor (GP) can be contacted at any time for yourself, your baby, or child. Many doctors will see small babies at the beginning of surgery hours or without an appointment if necessary, but be prepared to

---

Register your baby with your doctor
Register your baby with your doctor as early as possible with the pink card that you'll be given when you register your baby's birth at the local registry office. Sign the card and take or send it to your doctor. If you need the doctor to see your baby before you've registered the birth, you can go to the surgery and fill in a registration form for the doctor there.

If you move, register with a new doctor close to you as soon as possible. See page 124.

---

wait. Some will give advice over the phone. Some doctors provide developmental assessments and immunisation themselves, or you can go to a child health clinic.

CHILD HEALTH CLINICS

Your child health clinic offers regular health and development assessments (see page 33) and immunisation (see page 90) for your baby or child. It's run by health visitors and doctors. You can talk about any problems to do with your child, but if your child's ill and is likely to need treatment, you should go to your GP.

At some child health clinics you can get baby milk and vitamins cheaper than in the shops. If you're entitled to free baby milk and vitamins, or to low price baby milk, you may be able to get these at your clinic. Clinics are good places to meet other parents. Some run mother and baby or parent and toddler groups, and sell secondhand baby clothes and equipment.

COMMUNITY HEALTH COUNCILS

Your community health council (CHC in your phone book under the name of your health authority) can advise you on how to get what you need from the health services and on what you're entitled to. It can also give you information about local services. For example, if you want to change your doctor, your CHC will have a list of local doctors and may know something about them.

LOCAL AUTHORITY SERVICES

SOCIAL SERVICES DEPARTMENTS

Your social services department (in your phone book under the name of your local authority) can give you information about most services for parents and children: day nurseries, childminders, playgroups, opportunity groups (which include children with special needs), family centres, and so on. Many local authorities produce booklets listing local services for families with under fives. Ask at your local library, social services department, citizens advice bureau, or other advice centre.

SOCIAL WORKERS

Social workers are usually based in social services departments. Their job is to provide support for people in need in their area who're having difficulty coping, financially or practically. A social worker may be able to get your child a nursery place, help you find better housing, and give you information about your rights.

To contact a social worker phone your local social services department. Or ask your health visitor to put you in touch.

HOUSING DEPARTMENTS

The housing department (in your phone book under the name of your local authority) is responsible for all council housing in your area and will run the council housing waiting list.

The housing department has a legal duty to house people in certain priority groups who're homeless (or are soon going to be) through no fault of their own. Priority groups include pregnant women and parents of children under 16.

Through your housing department you should also be able to find out about local housing associations, which also provide housing for rent.

EDUCATION DEPARTMENTS

Your education department (in your phone book under the name of your local authority) is responsible for all the state-run nursery schools, nursery classes, and infant schools in your area and can give you information about them.

The education department also has a responsibility to assess children with special needs and provide suitable education for them (see page 37).

ADVICE CENTRES

Advice centres are any non-profit making agencies that give advice on benefits, housing, and other problems. They include citizens advice bureaux, community law centres, welfare rights offices, housing aid centres,

---

SCOTLAND AND NORTHERN IRELAND

Community health councils
In Scotland, community health councils are called local health councils. In Northern Ireland they are called health and social services councils. Look in your phone book under the name of your local health board, or local health and social services board.

Social services department
In Scotland, the social services department is called the social work department (in your phone book under the name of your local regional council). In Northern Ireland, it is called the Health and Social Services Board (in the phone book under Health and Social Services Board).

Housing department
In Scotland, you will find your housing department in your phone book under the name of your local district council. In Northern Ireland the housing department is called the Housing Executive (in the phone book under Northern Ireland Housing Executive).

Education department
In Scotland, you will find your education department in your phone book under the name of your local regional council. In Northern Ireland the education department is called the Education and Library Board (in the phone book under Education and Library Board). Note: in this publication, the NHS also refers to the Northern Ireland Health and Personal Social Services.

neighbourhood centres, and community projects. Look for them under these names in your phone book, or under the name of your local authority.

USING THE SERVICES

If you're to get the best from these services it helps to be clear about what you want.

- Before you meet with any professional, think through exactly what you want to talk about and what information you can give that'll be helpful. You may want to make some notes beforehand and take them with you as a reminder.
- Unless your child needs to be with you, try to get a friend or neighbour to look after him or her so that you can concentrate. It's much easier to talk and listen if you're not distracted.
- If you do have to go with your child or children, take books or toys with you to entertain them.
- Try to consider the answers or advice given to you. If your immediate feeling is 'but that wouldn't work for me' or 'that isn't what I'm looking for', then say so and try to talk about it. You're less likely to come away with an answer you're not happy with or can't put into practice.
- If a problem is making life difficult or is really worrying you, it's worth keeping going until you get some kind of answer, if not a solution. So if the first person you talk to can't help, ask if they can suggest where else you might go. Or if the doctor or health

visitor suggests a remedy that doesn't work, go back and ask again.

- Some professionals aren't good at explaining things. If you don't understand, then say so. It's their responsibility to be clear, not yours to guess what they meant. Go back over what's said to you to get it straight.
- If your first language is not English, you may be able to get the help of a *linkworker* or *health advocate*. Their job is not just to translate the words, but to act as a friend and make sure that the professionals understand just what you need. Ask your health visitors if there's a linkworker or health advocate in your area.

(A clinic doctor) "I know the services often let parents down or don't give them what they need. All I can say is, parents have got to keep asking for what they want. If they don't do that, either for their children or for themselves, no-one else will."

HOW TO CHANGE YOUR GP

You may need to change your GP if you move. You may want to change for other reasons, even if you're not moving house.

First find a GP who will accept you. See if anybody can recommend one. Your local community health council or family health services authority (FHSA) (in Scotland your local health board; in Northern Ireland the Central Services Agency in Belfast) keeps a list of doctors in

your area. You may have to try more than one GP before you find one willing to accept you, especially if you live in a heavily populated area. If you can't find someone after several attempts, your FHSA will do it for you and you should send them your medical card if you have it, or the name and address of your previous GP if not.

When you call at the surgery of the GP you've chosen, you may be asked why you want to change. You don't have to give a reason but if you do, try to avoid criticising your old GP. Say something good about the new one instead. For example, the surgery may be easier to get to, the hours may be better, the GP may have a good reputation for treating young children, the practice may be larger and provide more, or you may prefer a woman doctor, or one who shares your cultural background.

Once you've found a GP to accept you, leave your medical card with the receptionist. You don't have to contact your old GP at all. If you've lost your medical card, your new GP will probably ask you to complete a form instead, although sometimes you may be asked to contact the FHSA (in the phone book under the name of your health authority), giving the name and address of your previous GP, to obtain a medical card first. If you don't know your old GP's name and address, this may take a while, but if you need treatment in the meantime, you can approach any GP, who must take you on, at least temporarily. It's best to say from the beginning that you need treatment now if you're also asking to be permanently registered with that GP.

FINDING OTHER HELP

The help you want may not best come from the services or from professionals. There are many other sources of help available to parents – not only family and friends, but also many different kinds of local groups and voluntary organisations.

LOCAL GROUPS

To find out about local groups
- Ask your health visitor or GP.
- Ask at your citizens advice bureau or other advice centre, your local library, your social services department, or your local Council for Voluntary Service (in your phone book, maybe as Voluntary Action Group, Rural Community Council or Volunteer Bureau). (In Northern Ireland, the Council for Voluntary Service is called the Northern Ireland Council for Voluntary Action.

In Scotland, contact the Scottish Council for Voluntary Organisations.)
- Look on noticeboards in your child health clinic, health centre, GP's waiting room, local library, advice centres, supermarket, newsagent, toy shop.
- Look through the list of national organisations (pages 133–6). Many run local groups.

In many areas there are now groups offering support to parents who share the same background and culture. Many of these are women's or mothers' groups. Your health visitor may know if there's such a group in your area. Or ask at places like your local library, your citizens advice bureau, or other advice or community centre, your local Council for Voluntary Service, or your Community Relations Council (in your phone book, maybe as Council for Racial Equality or Community Relations Office).

STARTING A GROUP

If you can't find a local group that suits you or can't find the support you need, think about setting it up for yourself. Many local groups have begun through a couple of mothers (say with crying babies, or sleepless toddlers, or just fed up and lonely) getting together and talking. You could advertise on your clinic noticeboard or in a newsagent's window or local newspaper. Or ask your health visitor to put you in touch with others in the same situation as yourself. You don't have to offer any more than a place to meet and a few cups of coffee. Or you could get a copy of *New lives* (available from your health visitor or direct from the Maternity Alliance, see page 136), which has suggestions for how to set up a new mothers' group.

··

"I think looking after children is the hardest job going and the one you get least preparation for."

"The most important thing I do for them? Love them. I suppose sometimes they don't feel I love them – when I scream and shout. But I love them. And I try to show it."

"The thing is, you can't be perfect and the world's not perfect and they're not perfect either, no matter what you do. You can't change your children. You start off thinking you can control things, but you can't. You learn to accept a lot, being a parent."

"It took me a long, long time to get rid of the idea that every other mother in the world was a better mother than me. I think in the end it dawned on me that my own two children think I'm all right."

"The best thing is when they get to the age when they'll come to you and put their arms round you and give you a hug, just because they want to. That's the best feeling there is."

"Well I'll never be the same, that's for sure. And I'd not have it any different."

Rights and Benefits

The following pages are a guide to the main benefits available to families with young children. You may qualify for other benefits too. It's always worth checking that you're claiming everything to which you are entitled. See below for where to go to get advice.

WHERE TO GET ADVICE AND HELP

Working out what benefits you're entitled to and making claims can be complicated. Get help if you need it.

- You can go to your social security office (in the phone book under 'Social Security, Department of'; in Scotland under 'Social Security, Department of'; in Northern Ireland under 'Social Security Agency'). Or go to your local citizens advice bureau or other advice centre (see page 123); or, in Northern Ireland, to the Benefit Shop, Castle Court, Royal Avenue, Belfast. Many social security offices are very busy and an advice centre is often the best place to go.
- A social worker should be able to advise you. Phone your social services department (see page 123) and explain what help you want. Some local authorities also have welfare rights officers. Again, phone your social services department and ask.
- The Department of Social Services runs a free telephone service – Freeline Social Security. The service doesn't deal with claims, but should be able to answer any questions about benefits. Dial 0800 666555 (or, in Northern Ireland, the Social Security Agency on 0800 616757).
- Some voluntary organisations offer information and advice on benefits. See page 135 for details.

Rates of benefits are not given here as they change every year, but you can find them in leaflet NI196 (in Northern Ireland, NIL96), *Social security benefit rates*.

FOR PARENTS

CHILD BENEFIT

This is a tax-free payment made to virtually anybody responsible for a child under 16. You can also claim for a child aged between 16 and 19 who's in full-time education not above A-level or an equivalent standard. In addition Child Benefit may be extended for a few weeks for school leavers of 16 and 17 who register for work or youth training. (In Northern Ireland, register at an office of the Department of Economic Development.)

Leaflets giving general information
- **FB8 Babies and benefits.** A guide to benefits for expectant and new mothers.
- **FB27 Bringing up children?** A guide to benefits for families with children.
- **FB28 Sick or disabled?** A guide to benefits if you're sick or disabled for a few days or more.
- **FB2 Which benefit?** A short guide to all social security benefits.

Government leaflets giving more information about particular benefits are listed under each benefit. You can get these leaflets:
- **from your local social security office**
- **from some large post offices**
- **from your citizens advice bureau or other advice centre**
- **by writing to the DSS Leaflets Unit, PO Box 21, Stanmore, Middlesex HA7 1AY (in Northern Ireland, this option does not apply)**
- **by phoning Freeline Social Security on 0800 666555 or, in Northern Ireland, 0800 616757.**

Child Benefit is paid:
- for each child you are responsible for (you don't have to be the parent to claim);
- every four weeks by a book of orders, which you cash at the post office, or direct into most banks or building society accounts. (If you are a one-parent family or on Family Credit or Income Support (see pages 129–30) you can choose to be paid weekly.)

How to claim

To claim Child Benefit for a new baby, use the coupon in leaflet FB8 *Babies and benefits* to get a claim form. (In Northern Ireland, use the Child Benefit claim pack, available from the Child Benefit Office, Castle Court, Royal Avenue, Belfast.) Otherwise ask your social security office. If you claim late you can be paid in arrears for up to six months.

If you're a couple (married or unmarried) the child's mother should claim. If a couple separates and lives with other partners one of the child's natural parents should claim.

Leaflets
FB27 Bringing up children?
CH1 Child Benefit
CH4 Child Benefit for children away from home
CH5 Child Benefit for people entering Britain (in Northern Ireland, Child Benefit for people coming to live in Northern Ireland)
CH6 Child Benefit for people leaving Britain (in Northern Ireland, Child Benefit for people leaving Northern Ireland)

ONE PARENT BENEFIT

This is a tax-free addition to Child Benefit made to anybody bringing up a child on their own, whether or not they're the child's natural parent. You can't claim if you're living with someone as husband or wife.

One Parent Benefit is paid with your Child Benefit for the eldest dependent child and entitlement continues so long as you've a dependent child.

The amount paid is the same whatever your income or savings or however many children.

You can't get One Parent Benefit if you're getting other benefits such as Widowed Mother's Allowance, Guardian's Allowance, or Invalid Care Allowance for the same child.

One Parent Benefit doesn't affect Family Credit (see page 129), but any Income Support (see page 129) you get may be reduced by the amount of your One Parent Benefit.

How to claim

Claim One Parent Benefit with the form in leaflet CH11 *One Parent Benefit* (in Northern Ireland, *A guide to One Parent Benefit*) or use the coupon in FB8 *Babies and benefits* to get a claim form. If you have not yet claimed Child Benefit, claim it now.

Leaflets
FB27 Bringing up children?
CH11 One Parent Benefit (in Northern Ireland, A guide to One Parent Benefit)
NP45 A guide to widow's benefits
NI14 Guardian's Allowance (in Northern Ireland, NIL14 Guardian's Allowance)

FOR PREGNANT WOMEN

NEW RIGHTS AND BENEFITS

This information applies to women whose babies are due *on or after 16 October 1994* when new regulations for both maternity pay and leave come into force. All employed women will have a right to take 14 weeks maternity leave and benefit rules will be changed. (NB If your baby is due before 16 October, you must have worked for two years full-time or five years part-time to qualify for the higher rate SMP and the right to return to your job. If you have worked for at least six months by the qualifying week, you will qualify for lower rate SMP. Check with your local DSS or the Maternity Alliance (see page 136 for details.)

STATUTORY MATERNITY PAY (SMP)

This is a payment for pregnant women in employment in the following circumstances.
- If you've have worked for the same employer for at least 26 weeks by the 15th week before the week your baby is due. You must have worked at least one day in the 15th week. If the 15th week is your 26th week of employment then you must work the whole week. To work out which is the 15th week before your baby is due, look on the calendar for the Sunday before (or on) which your baby is due. *Not* counting that Sunday, count back 15 Sundays. The 15th week before your baby is due begins on that Sunday.

→

To get
SMP
you
must
have
worked
at
least 1
day in
this
week

SUNDAY
MONDAY
TUESDAY
WEDNESDAY
THURSDAY
FRIDAY
SATURDAY

SUNDAY
MONDAY
TUESDAY
WEDNESDAY
THURSDAY
FRIDAY
SATURDAY 15

SUNDAY
MONDAY
TUESDAY
WEDNESDAY
THURSDAY
FRIDAY
SATURDAY 14

SUNDAY
MONDAY
TUESDAY
WEDNESDAY
THURSDAY
FRIDAY
SATURDAY 13

SUNDAY
MONDAY
TUESDAY
WEDNESDAY
THURSDAY
FRIDAY
SATURDAY 12

SUNDAY
MONDAY
TUESDAY
WEDNESDAY
THURSDAY
FRIDAY
SATURDAY 11

SUNDAY
MONDAY
TUESDAY
WEDNESDAY
THURSDAY
FRIDAY
SATURDAY 10

SUNDAY
MONDAY
TUESDAY
WEDNESDAY
THURSDAY
FRIDAY
SATURDAY 9

SUNDAY
MONDAY
TUESDAY
WEDNESDAY
THURSDAY
FRIDAY
SATURDAY 8

SUNDAY
MONDAY
TUESDAY
WEDNESDAY
THURSDAY
FRIDAY
SATURDAY 7

SUNDAY
MONDAY
TUESDAY
WEDNESDAY
THURSDAY
FRIDAY
SATURDAY 6

SUNDAY
MONDAY
TUESDAY
WEDNESDAY
THURSDAY
FRIDAY
SATURDAY 5

SUNDAY
MONDAY
TUESDAY
WEDNESDAY
THURSDAY
FRIDAY
SATURDAY 4

SUNDAY
MONDAY
TUESDAY
WEDNESDAY
THURSDAY
FRIDAY
SATURDAY 3

SUNDAY
MONDAY
TUESDAY
WEDNESDAY
THURSDAY
FRIDAY
SATURDAY 2

SUNDAY
MONDAY
TUESDAY
WEDNESDAY
THURSDAY
FRIDAY
SATURDAY 1

SUNDAY
MONDAY
TUESDAY
WEDNESDAY
THURSDAY
FRIDAY
SATURDAY *

↑

count
back
the
weeks

Suppose
this is
the date
your
baby is
due

→

See the example on the calendar here.

● Your average weekly earnings (normally the amount you have actually earned in the 19th to 26th weeks of your pregnancy) must have been at or above the amount where you start paying National Insurance contributions.

SMP payments

● SMP is paid for 18 weeks. The first six weeks will be 90 per cent of your average weekly earnings, followed by 12 weeks at the lower rate of SMP.

● SMP is paid by your employer, either weekly or monthly, depending on how you're normally paid. Tax and National Insurance contributions may be deducted.

● You can choose when to start getting your SMP. The earliest you can start getting your SMP is 11 weeks before the week the baby is due. The latest date your maternity pay period can start is the week following the week in which you give birth, so you can work right up to the birth without losing any of your 18 weeks maternity pay.

● SMP is paid regardless of whether you intend to return to work after your baby is born.

How to claim

Write to your employer at least 21 days before you intend to stop work because of your pregnancy. Enclose your maternity certificate (form MAT B1 (in Northern Ireland, form MB1)), which is given to you by your doctor or midwife when you are about 26 weeks pregnant. If you don't get your maternity certificate in time,

write to your employer anyway and send the form later. You may lose your right to SMP if you don't give 21 days' notice.

If you're unsure whether you can get SMP, ask your employer anyway. If you can't get SMP you may be able to claim Maternity Allowance (see below).

Leaflets
FB8 Babies and benefits
NI17A Maternity benefits (in Northern Ireland, NIL17A)

MATERNITY ALLOWANCE

This is a benefit for pregnant women who've recently given up a job or who work, but don't qualify for Statutory Maternity Pay (SMP) or who are self-employed.

You can claim it if you're not entitled to SMP (see above) but have worked and paid standard rate National Insurance contributions for at least 26 of the 66 weeks ending in the week before your baby is due.

Maternity Allowance payments

● There will be two rates of Maternity Allowance. A *lower* rate will be paid to *self-employed women and those who have recently become unemployed*. A *higher rate* will be paid to *women who are employed in the 15th week before the expected week of childbirth*.

● Maternity Allowance is paid for up to 18 weeks in the same way as SMP (see facing page). Payments start no earlier than 11 weeks before the week your baby is due.

● It's paid only for weeks when you're not working.

- It's paid by a book of orders that you can cash at the post office.

How to claim

Get form MA1 (in Northern Ireland, form MB1) from your antenatal clinic or your social security office along with your maternity certificate , given to you by your doctor or midwife when you are about 26 weeks pregnant. If you're claiming Maternity Allowance because you have been refused SMP, get form SMP1 from your employer and send this with your claim.

Claim as early as possible after the start of the 14th week before your baby is due. If you have not paid 26 weeks National Insurance contributions by this time, then you may decide to work later into your pregnancy; and you should send off the MA1 form as soon as you have made 26 National Insurance contributions. You may lose benefit if you claim after the birth.

If you've worked in the last couple of years and paid National Insurance contributions, it's worth claiming Maternity Allowance *even if you don't appear to qualify for it*. You may still be able to get Sickness Benefit if you've paid enough National Insurance contributions in earlier tax years. If you claim Maternity Allowance, but don't qualify for it, you should automatically be considered for Sickness Benefit. Sickness Benefit is paid from the 6th week before the baby is due until two weeks after the baby is born.

Leaflets
FB8 Babies and benefits
NI17A Maternity benefits (in Northern Ireland, NIL17A)

OTHER BENEFITS

When pregnant, and for a year after your baby is born.
- Free NHS prescriptions. To claim during pregnancy ask your midwife for form FW8 as soon as you're sure that you're pregnant. If you've had your baby and didn't claim while pregnant, use the claim form in P11 *NHS prescriptions.*
- Free NHS dental treatment. To claim, simply tell your dentist that you're pregnant or have a baby under one year old.
- You may be able to get a Maternity Payment from the Social Fund (see page 131).
- If you're on Income Support (see page 130), you can get free milk and vitamins while you're pregnant or have a child under five.

FOR FAMILIES

FAMILY CREDIT

This a tax-free benefit for working families with children. It's not a loan and doesn't have to be paid back. To be able to get Family Credit you, or your partner, must be working at least 16 hours a week and you must have at least one child under 16 (or under 19 in full-time education up to or including A-level or an equivalent standard).

You can qualify for Family Credit whether you're employed or self-employed or whether you're a two-parent or one-parent family. You may be single,

married, or living with a partner as if you were married. Your right to Family Credit, and how much you get, depends on you and your partner's net income, how many children you have and what age they are, and what savings you and your partner have.

Family Credit payments
- Family Credit is normally paid for 26 weeks at a time. In each 26-week period, the amount you get stays the same even if your earnings or other circumstances change during that time.
- It is normally paid weekly by a book of orders, which you can cash at the post office or, if you prefer, every four weeks directly into your bank and building society account.

How to claim

Use the *Family Credit claim pack* FC1. Fill in the claim form and send to the Family Credit Unit (or, in Northern Ireland, the Family Credit Branch) in the envelope provided.

Other benefits if you get Family Credit
- Free NHS prescriptions.
- Free NHS dental treatment.
- NHS vouchers for glasses.
- Free travel to hospital for NHS treatment.
- You may also be able to get payments from the Social Fund (see page 131). For example, a Maternity Payment to help buy new things for a baby.
- If you've a child under one year old who's not being breastfed, you can get powdered baby milk at a reduced price. Take your Family Credit order book (or notice of award of benefit if you're paid directly into your

bank or building society account) to your local baby clinic to prove that you're getting Family Credit.

Leaflets
FCI Family Credit claim pack
ABII Help with NHS costs

INCOME SUPPORT

This is a benefit for anybody who doesn't have enough money to live on and has less than £8,000 in savings.

To be able to get Income Support you must be aged 18 or over (or 16–17 if it is 11 weeks before your baby is due or if you have a child or face severe hardship) and you (or you partner, if you have one) must be out of work or not working 16 hours or more a week.

How much Income Support you get depends on your age, whether you have a partner or dependents, your income, other benefits you are getting (such as Child Benefit or One Parent Benefit), and how much you have in savings. Your right to Income Support doesn't depend on your National Insurance contributions.

Depending on your circumstances, Income Support payments can be made up of:
● a personal allowance for yourself and your partner (if you have one), and an allowance for any child or young person that you look after;
● premium payments for people who have special expenses (such as families with children, lone parents, and parents of children with disabilities);
● housing cost payments to cover certain costs (eg help with mortgage interest payments not met by Housing Benefit), see below.

How to claim

If you're unemployed, ask for an Income Support claim form at your unemployment benefit office (social security office in Northern Ireland). Anyone else should fill in the coupon in leaflet IS1 *Income Support*. If you send this coupon to your social security office, they'll send you a detailed postal claim form for you to fill in.

Other benefits if you get Income Support

● Housing Benefit (if you pay rent; or, in Northern Ireland, to help with rent and/or rates).
● Council Tax Benefit (see opposite); this does not apply in Northern Ireland.
● Free NHS prescriptions.
● Free NHS dental treatment.
● NHS vouchers for glasses.
● Free travel to hospital for NHS treatment.
● If you get Income Support and are pregnant or have a child under five, you can get tokens for free milk. Free vitamins for yourself or your child are also available. Ask your doctor or midwife for form FW8 as soon as you're pregnant. Take or send it to your social security office. If you have a baby under one year, tokens can be exchanged for special baby milk or ordinary doorstep milk.
● You may also be able to get payments from the Social Fund (see page 131). For example, a Maternity Payment to help buy new things for a baby.

Leaflets
ABII Help with NHS costs
ISI Income Support
SB20 A guide to Income Support (in Northern Ireland, IS20)
SB22 Income Support – new rules (not applicable in Northern Ireland)

HOUSING BENEFIT

Most people on Income Support and other people on low incomes can get help with their rent. You can't get Housing Benefit if your savings are more than £16,000. If you pay rent to the council your Housing Benefit is paid directly to them and your bills will be smaller. If you pay rent to a private landlord then your Housing Benefit is paid directly to you. If you're on Income Support you'll usually get most or all of your rent (not including service charges) paid, but other low income families may get less depending on how many people are in the family, what their income is, and how much the rent is. Your benefit will be reduced if you have more than £3000 in savings.

In Northern Ireland, Housing Benefit for tenants is administered by the Northern Ireland Housing Executive (NIHE) and by the Rate Collection Agency (RCA) for owner-occupiers. If you claim Income Support you will get a Housing Benefit claim form from your social security office. If you are not claiming Income Support, you should obtain a claim form from your NIHE district office (tenants), or RCA local office (if you own your own home).

How to claim

People on Income Support can claim Housing Benefit on form NHB1 (in Northern Ireland, form HB1) when they claim Income Support. Get a form from your local council (or, in Northern Ireland, from your local Northern Ireland Housing Executive Office or Rate Collection Agency Office) if you don't get Income Support.

COUNCIL TAX BENEFIT (NOT APPLICABLE IN NORTHERN IRELAND)

This benefit helps people on Income Support or on a low income to pay their Council Tax. You can't get Council Tax Benefit if your savings are more than £16,000.

Most people on Income Support can get 100% of the Council Tax paid in benefit. For other low income families, how much benefit you get depends on your income and savings, and whether other adults live with you.

How to claim

If you get Housing Benefit you'll automatically be assessed for Council Tax Benefit. Otherwise you'll need to get a claim form from your council offices.

HELP WITH NATIONAL HEALTH SERVICE COSTS

NHS BENEFITS FOR ALL CHILDREN UNDER 16

- Free NHS prescriptions.
- Free NHS dental treatment.
- NHS vouchers for glasses.

YOUNG PEOPLE UNDER 19 AND STILL IN FULL-TIME EDUCATION

Young people under 19 and still in full-time education get free prescriptions, free dental treatment, and vouchers for glasses. Those over 16, but not in full-time education get free dental treatment until they are 18.

NHS BENEFITS FOR ALL PREGNANT WOMEN AND MOTHERS OF BABIES UNDER ONE YEAR OLD

- Free NHS prescriptions.
- Free NHS dental treatment.

For how to claim see 'For pregnant women' page 127.

NHS BENEFITS IF YOU GET FAMILY CREDIT OR INCOME SUPPORT

- Free NHS prescriptions.
- Free NHS dental treatment.
- NHS vouchers for glasses.
- Free travel to hospital for NHS treatment.
- If you get income support and are pregnant or have a child under five, you can also get tokens for free milk. Free vitamins for yourself and your child are also available.(Look under 'Income Support' page 130 for how to claim.)
- If you get Family Credit and have a child under one year old, you can get baby milk at a reduced price (look under 'Family Credit' page 129 for how to claim).

IF YOU DON'T GET FAMILY CREDIT OR INCOME SUPPORT BUT YOUR INCOME IS LOW

You may still get some help with NHS costs. To find out if you qualify for help, get form AG1 *Help with NHS costs* (from hospitals, dentists, and opticians as well as social security offices). Fill it in and send it to the Agency Benefits Unit in the pre-paid envelope provided with the form. (The Agency Benefits Unit doesn't exist in Northern Ireland: you should use your social security office.) The Unit will check your circumstances. If you qualify for help, you'll be sent a certificate of entitlement, setting out the amount of help you can get for each type of charge. The certificate is valid for six months.

If your circumstances change, write to the Agency Benefits Unit (or, in Northern Ireland, to your local social security office). They'll issue a fresh certificate if necessary.

Leaflets
AB11 Help with NHS costs
P11 NHS prescriptions
D11 NHS dental treatment
G11 NHS vouchers for glasses
H11 NHS hospital travel costs
WF11 NHS wigs and fabric support
FB28 Sick or disabled?

THE SOCIAL FUND

The Social Fund offers help with certain expenses that are difficult to meet out of your regular income.

- If you or your partner are getting Income Support or Family Credit (see page 129), you may be able to get a Maternity Payment to help buy things for your new baby. You can claim a Maternity Payment after the 29th week of pregnancy, up until the time your baby is three months old. If you're adopting a baby you can apply for Maternity Payment as long as that baby is not more than 12 months old when that application is made. The application must be made within three months of adoption. Any savings over £500 will affect the amount of Maternity Payment. Get claim form SF100 from an antenatal clinic or social security office.

- If you have a child under five years old and you're getting Income Support, you'll automatically get a Cold Weather Payment for any consecutive seven-day period when the temperature averages 0°C or below. If you don't receive your payment, submit a written claim and ask for a decision.

- If you're getting Income Support, you may be able to get a Community Care Grant. These non-repayable payments are given to help, for example, people with disabilities lead independent lives in the community. Sometimes grants are given to families under exceptional stress. Grants may be made for items such as furniture and house repairs. Any savings of over £500 will affect the amount of Community Care Grant. Get form SF300 from your social security office.

- If you've been getting Income Support for 26 weeks or more, you may be able to get a Budgeting Loan. These are interest-free loans made to help spread payment for certain expenses over a longer period. Loans may be made for items such as essential household equipment, safety

equipment (such as a fireguard), furniture (such as bedding), repairs, and maintenance. The amount of the loan is decided by the Social Fund officer, according to your needs. The loan has to be repaid. Any savings over £500 will affect the amount of a Budgeting Loan. Get form SF300 from your social security office.

- In an emergency, if you can't afford something that's urgently needed, you may be able to get a Crisis Loan. These loans can cover living expenses for up to 14 days, or such things as essential household equipment or travel costs. Crisis Loans are only given if there's no other way of avoiding risk to somebody's health or safety. The amount of the loan is decided by the Social Fund officer. The loan has to be repaid.

For more information, contact a social security office.

Leaflets
SB16 A guide to the Social Fund (in Northern Ireland, S16)

FOR CHILDREN WITH SPECIAL NEEDS

If you've a disabled child who's needed a lot of extra looking after for at least three months, you may be able to get Disability Living Allowance. Leaflet DLA1 *Disability Living Allowance* gives more information and includes a claim form.

Income Support can be increased if you get Disability Living Allowance for a dependent child. Income Support is also increased if you receive Invalid Care Allowance.

If your child gets either the middle or the higher rate of the care component of Disability Living Allowance and you spend a lot of time looking after him or her, you may be able to get Invalid Care Allowance. You must be giving care for at least 35 hours a week and be earning less than a certain amount. DS700 *Invalid Care Allowance claims pack* tells you how to claim.

If your child has difficulty walking or needs supervision and guidance outside, you can claim the mobility component of Disability Living Allowance three months before his or her fifth birthday.

THE FAMILY FUND

The Family Fund is a government fund run by the Joseph Rowntree Foundation. It gives cash grants to families caring for severely mentally or physically disabled children under 16. Grants are made to meet special needs not met by the health or social services, for example, a washing machine, special equipment, clothing, bedding, holiday expenses. Family income and circumstances are taken into account when applications are considered, but there's no means test. Write to the address on page 135 for more information and an application form.

USEFUL ORGANISATIONS

Some of these organisations are large; many are small. Some organisations have local branches; some can put you in touch with local groups.

Organisations marked * produce publications. When you write, it's usually a good idea to send a large stamped addressed envelope for a reply.

ADDICTIVE DRUGS

Narcotics Anonymous
PO Box 417
London SW10 0DP
(0171) 498 9005
Self-help organisations whose members help each other to stay clear of drugs. Write or phone between 12pm and 8pm for information and the address of your local group. Some groups have a crèche.*

SCODA (The Standing Conference on Drug Abuse)
1–4 Hatton Place
London EC1N 8ND
(0171) 430 2341
Information and local treatment and services for drug users, family and friends.*

Scottish Drug Forum
5 Oswald Street
Glasgow G1 4QR
(0141) 221 1175
Coordinate and give information about local services.

ALCOHOL

Alcohol Concern
Waterbridge House
32–36 Loman Street
London, SE1 0EE
(0171) 928 7377
For information on local alcohol councils offering advice, information, and support.*

Scottish Council on Alcohol
137–145 Sauchiehall Street
Glasgow G2 3EW
(0141) 333 9677
For information about local councils on alcohol; promotes safer, healthier drinking styles; educates on alcohol-related problems.

BEHAVIOURAL DIFFICULTIES

CRY-SIS Support Group
BM CRY-SIS
London WC1N 3XX
(0171) 404 5011
(8am–11pm 7 days per week)
Self help and support for families with excessively crying, sleepless and demanding children.*

Enuresis Resource and Information Centre
Institute of Child Health
65 St Michael's Hill
Bristol BS2 8DZ
(0117) 9264920
Provides advice and information to children, young adults, parents, and professionals on bed-wetting.

The Hyperactive Children's Support Group
Mrs S Bunday
71 Whyke Lane
Chichester PO19 2LD
(01903) 725182
(10am–3pm Tuesday–Friday)
Information to help problems related to hyperactivity and allergy.*

BREASTFEEDING

Association of Breastfeeding Mothers
Sydenham Green Health Centre
26 Holmshaw Close
London SE26 4TH
(0181) 778 4769
24-hour telephone advice service for breastfeeding mothers. Local support groups.*

La Leche League (Great Britain)
BM 3424
London WC1N 3XX,
(0171) 242 1278
Help and information for women who want to breastfeed. Personal counselling. Local groups. Write with SAE for details of your nearest counsellor/group.*

CHILDCARE/ PLAY AND DEVELOPMENT

Child Growth Foundation
2 Mayfield Avenue, Chiswick
London W4 1PW
(0181) 994 7625/995 0257
Information and advice for parents concerned about their child's growth.*

National Association for Maternal and Child Welfare (NAMCW)
40/42 Osnaburgh Street
London NW1 3ND
(0171) 383 4117
(0171) 383 1315 (Publications dept),
(0171) 383 4541 (Education dept)
Advice and courses on child care and family life.*

National Childcare Campaign/Daycare Trust
Wesley House
4 Wild Court
London WC2B 5AU
(0171) 405 5617/8
Campaigns for the provision of good childcare facilities. The Daycare Trust gives information on all aspects of childcare.*

National Childminding Association
National Development Officer Room 7
Stirling Business Centre Wellgreen
Stirling FK8 2DZ
(01786) 445377
An organisation for childminders, childcare workers, parents, and anyone with an interest in pre-school care. Works to improve status and conditions of childminders and standards of childcare.*

Parents at Work
77 Holloway Road
London N7 8JZ
(0171) 700 5771
Information and advice on childcare provision for working parents. Local groups.*

Play Matters/The National Association of Toy and Leisure
68 Churchway
London NW1 1LT
(0171) 387 9592
Information about local toy libraries (which lend toys). For all families with babies and young children, including those with special needs. Runs ACTIVE groups, which provides aids, information and workshops for children with disabilities.

Pre-school Playgroups Association
14 Elliot Place
Glasgow G3 8EP
(0141) 221 4148
Help and advice on setting up and running parent and toddler groups and playgroups. Contact with local playgroups.

Working for Childcare
77 Holloway Road
London N7 8JZ
(0171) 700 0281
Advice and information for employers, trade unions, and others on workplace childcare.

CONTRACEPTION

Family Planning Association
27–35 Mortimer Street
London W1N 7RJ
(0171) 636 7866
Information and advice on all aspects of family planning and contraception.*

Family Planning Brook Advisory Centres
Brook Central Office
153A East Street
London SE17 2SD
(0171) 708 1234
Advice and practical help with contraception and pregnancy testing, advice on unplanned pregnancies and sexual counselling for young men and women. Free and confidential. For your nearest centre look in the local phone book or contact Brook Central Office.*

DEPRESSION AND STRESS

Association for Postnatal Illness (APNI)
25 Jerdan Place
London SW6 1BE
(0171) 386 0868
(between 10am and 2pm)
Support for mothers suffering from postnatal depression.*

MAMA (Meet-a-Mum Association)
Drop-in Centre
17 Hilton Village
Oldtown Road
Inverness IV2 4HT
(01463) 234224
Support and help for women suffering from postnatal depression, feeling isolated and tired after having a baby, or just in need of a friend to share problems. Local groups and one-to-one contacts. Write with SAE for details of local groups.

MIND (National Association for Mental Health)
Granta House
15–19 Broadway
Stratford
London E15 4BQ
(0181) 519 2122
Help for people with mental illness. Also advice and information about coming off anti-depressants, tranquillisers, etc. Local associations.

Parentline
Westbury House
57 Hart Road
Thundersley Essex SS7 3PD
(01268) 757007
Support for troubled parents in times of stress or crisis, chiefly through a confidential and anonymous telephone helpline.

Scottish Association for Mental Health
Atlantic House
38 Gardner's Crescent
Edinburgh EH3 8DQ
(0131) 229 9687/228 5185
Network of local associations throughout Scotland.

HOUSING

Shelter
8 Hampton Terrace
Edinburgh EH12 5JD
(0131) 313 1550
Help for those who are homeless and advice on any kind of housing problem.*

ILLNESS AND DISABILITY (GENERAL)

Action for Sick Children (NAWCH Scotland)
Mrs O Young
15 Smith's Place
Edinburgh EH6 8HT
(0131) 553 6553
Support for sick children and their families – helping parents to be with their child in hospital and informing families about hospital care.*

Contact a Family
170 Tottenham Court Road
London W1P OHA
(0171) 383 3555
Links families of children with special needs through contact lines. All disabilities. Local parent support groups.*

Disability Scotland
Princes House
5 Shandwick Place
Edinburgh EH2 4RG
(0131) 229 8632
Information and advice on all aspects of disability, especially equipment and daily living problems. Referral to other organisations for adults and children with disabilities.*

MENCAP (Royal Society for Mentally Handicapped Children and Adults)
Mencap National Centre
117–123 Golden Lane
London EC1Y 0RT
(0171) 454 0454
Information, support, and advice for parents of children with mental handicaps. Local branches.*

National Disability Advice Line 0800 882200

ILLNESS AND DISABILITY (SPECIALISED)

Advisory Centre for Education (ACE) Ltd
Unit 1B
Aberdeen Studios
22–24 Highbury Grove
London N5 2EA
(0171) 354 8318
(Business Line)
(0171) 354 8321
(Free advice line 2pm–5pm Mon–Fri)
Independent education advice service for parents and children with special needs.*

AFASIC – Association for All Speech Impaired Children
347 Central Markets
Smithfield
EC1A 9NH
(0171) 236 3632/6487
Helps children with speech and language disorders. Information and advice for parents.*

Scottish Spina Bifida Association
190 Queensferry Road
Edinburgh EH4 2BW
(0131) 332 0743
Support for parents of children with spina bifida and/or hydrocephalus. Advice, practical and financial help. Local groups.*

Association of Parents of Vaccine Damaged Children
Mrs H Scott
21 Saughton Mains Gardens
Edinburgh EH11 3QG
(0131) 443 9287
Advises parents on claiming vaccine damage payment.

Body Positive
37–39 Montrose Terrace
Edinburgh EH7 5DJ
(0131) 652 0754
Offers counselling and support services to those affected by HIV and AIDS, their families, partners and friends.

British Diabetic Association
10 Queen Anne Street
London W1M 0BD
(0171) 323 1531
Information and support for all diabetics.*

CLAPA – Cleft Lip and Palate Association
Dental Department
Hospital for Sick Children
Great Ormond Street
London WC1N 3JH
(0171) 829 8614
Information and counselling for parents of newborn babies. Local groups.*

Coeliac Society of the United Kingdom
PO Box 220
High Wycombe
Bucks HP11 2HY
(01494) 437278
(9.30am–3pm)
Helps parents of children diagnosed as having the coeliac condition or dermatitis herpetiformis.

Council for Disabled Children
8 Wakley Street
Islington London
EC1V 7QE
(0171) 843600
Information for parents and details of all organisations offering help with particular handicaps.

Cystic Fibrosis Research Trust
Mr D Arthur
Inverallan
26 West Argyll Street
Helensburgh
Dumbarton G84 8DB
(01436) 676791
Support for the parents of children with cystic fibrosis. Local groups.*

Down's Syndrome Association (DSA)
158–160 Balgreen Road
Edinburgh EH11 3AU
(0131) 313 4225
Practical support, advice and information for parents of children with Down's syndrome.*

Enable (Scottish Society for the Mentally Handicapped)
13 Elmbank Street
Glasgow G2 4QA
(0141) 226 4541
A comprehensive information and support service for people with learning difficulties.

Haemophilia Society
123 Westminster Bridge Road
London SE1 7HR
(0171) 928 2020
Information, advice and practical help for families affected by haemophilia.*

Meningitis Research
Old Gloucester Road
Alveston
Bristol BS12 2LQ
(01454) 413344 (24 hours)
Provides updated information to the medical profession and advice, support, and counselling to the general public.

Muscular Dystrophy Group
7–11 Prescott Place
London SW4 6BS
(0171) 720 8055
Support and advice through local branches and a network of Family Care Officers.

National AIDS Helpline
0800 567123
Calls are confidential, free and available 24 hours a day. There is a Minicom on 0800 521361 for people who are deaf or hard of hearing. Information in other languages: Bengali, Gujerati, Hindi, Punjabi, Urdu and English on Wednesdays 6pm–10pm on 0800 282445. Cantonese and English on Tuesdays 6pm–10pm on 0800 282446. Arabic and English on Wednesdays 6pm–10pm on 0800 282447. Leaflets can be ordered in all these languages.*

National Asthma Campaign
Providence House
Providence Place
London N1 0NT
(0171) 226 2260
Asthma helpline
(0345) 010203
(Mon–Fri 9am–9pm)
Information and support for people with asthma, their families and health professionals. Booklets, videos and helpline. Over 180 nationwide branches.*

National Autistic Society
276 Willesden Lane
London NW2 5RB
(0181) 451 1114
Provides day and residential centres for the care and education of autistic children. Puts parents in touch with one another. Information and advice.

National Deaf Children's Society (NDCS)
45 Hereford Road
London W2 5AH
(0171) 229 9272
NDCS Technology Information Centre
4 Church Road
Edgbaston
Birmingham B15 3TD
(0121) 454 5151
0800 424545
(freephone 1pm–5pm)
Works for deaf children and their families. Information and advice on all aspects of childhood deafness. Local self-help groups.*

National Eczema Society (NES)
4 Tavistock Place
London WCIH 9RA
(0171) 388 4097
Support and information for people with eczema and their families. Nationwide network of local contacts offering practical advice and support.*

National Meningitis Trust
Fern House
Bath Road
Stroud GL5 3TJ
(01453) 751738
(01453) 751049 (24 hour helpline)
Information and support for those already affected by meningitis. Local groups.

Research Trust for Metabolic Diseases in Children (RTMDC)
Golden Gates Lodge
Weston Road
Crewe CWI IXN
(01270) 250221 (office hours) or (01270) 626834, (01244) 881605
Makes grants and allowances for the medical treatment and care of children with metabolic diseases. Puts parents in touch with each other.

Royal National Institute for the Blind (RNIB)
10 Magdala Crescent
Edinburgh EH12 5BE
Information, advice and services for blind people.

Scottish Council for Spastics
External Therapy & Advisory Services
ETAS Centre
II Ellersley Road
Edinburgh EH12 6HY
(0131) 313 5510

Scottish Society for Autistic Children
24D Barony Street
Edinburgh EH3 6NY
(0131) 557 0474
Provides day and residential centres for the care and education of autistic children. Puts parents in touch with one another. Information and advice.*

Scottish Spina Bifida Associations
190 Queensferry Road
Edinburgh EH4 2BW
(0131) 332 0743
Support for parents of children with spina bifida and/or hydrocephalus. Advice; practical and financial help. Local groups.*

SENSE (National Deaf-Blind and Rubella Association)
Head Office
Unit 5/2
8 Elliot Place
Clydeway Centre
Glasgow G3 8EP
(0141) 221 7577 (voice)
Advice and support for families of deaf-blind and rubella handicapped children.*

Sickle Cell Society
54 Station Road
Harlesden
London NW10 4UA
(0181) 961 7795/8346
Information, advice and counselling for families affected by sickle cell disease or trait. Financial help when needed.

Spastics Society
12 Park Crescent
London WIN 4EQ
(0171) 636 5020
Offers advice and support to parents of children with cerebral palsy.*

The Toxoplasmosis Trust
Room 26
61–71 Collier Street
London NI 9BE
(0171) 713 0599 (Helpline)
(0171) 713 0663 (Office)
Information and advice for pregnant women and support and counselling for sufferers and their families.

The UK Thalassaemia Society
107 Nightingale Lane
London N8 7QY
(0181) 348 0437
Information, and advice for families affected by thalassaemia.*

LONE PARENTS

Gingerbread
304 Maryhill Road
Glasgow G20 7YE
(0141) 353 0953
Self-help association for one-parent families. Local groups offer support, friendship, information, advice, and practical help.

LOSS AND BEREAVEMENT

Compassionate Friends
53 North Street
Bristol BS3 IEN
(0117) 9539639
An organisation of and for bereaved parents. Advice and support. Local groups.*

The Foundation for the Study of Infant Deaths (Cot Death Research and Support)
35 Belgrave Square
London SWIX 8QB
(0171) 235 0965/1721
Support and information for parents bereaved by a sudden infant death.*

Scottish Cot Death Trust
Royal Hospital for Sick Children
Yorkhill
Glasgow G3 8SJ
(0141) 357 3946
Support and information for parents bereaved by sudden infant death. Puts parents in touch with local support groups of other bereaved parents.*

Stillbirth and Neonatal Death Society (SANDS)
28 Portland Place
London WIN 4DE
(0171) 436 5881
Information and a national network of support groups for bereaved parents. Phone or write for details.*

RELATIONSHIPS

RELATE: Marriage Guidance
Herbert Gray College
Little Church Street
Rugby CV21 3AP
(01788) 573241
Confidential counselling on relationship problems of any kind. To find your local branch look under RELATE or Marriage Guidance in the phone book or contact the above addresses.

RIGHTS AND BENEFITS/ ACCESS TO SERVICES

Child Poverty Action Group
Scottish Regional Representative
Fife Money Advice Project
Unit 6
Wooding Business Centre
Cowdenbeath
Fife KY4 8HG
(01383) 610303
Campaigns on behalf of low-income families. Provides advisors with information and advice for parents on benefits, housing, welfare rights, etc.*

Child Support Agency
PO Box 55
Brierley Hill
West Midlands
DY5 IYL
(0345) 133133 (enquiry line)
The Government agency that assesses maintenance levels for parents who no longer live with their children. The agency will claim maintenance on behalf of the parent with care of the children but if you are on benefits the money claimed will be deducted from your benefit.

Citizens Advice Bureaux
26 George Square
Edinburgh EH8 9LD
(0131) 667 0156
For advice on all benefits, housing, your rights generally, and many other problems. To find your local CAB look in the phone book, ask at your local library, or

contact one of the head offices for the address. There may also be other advice centres in your area offering similar help.

Community Relations Councils (CRCs)
Commission for Racial Equality
10–12 Allington Street
London SWIE 5EH
(0171) 828 7022
Sometimes called Councils for Racial Equality or Community Relations Offices. They are concerned with community relations in their area and often know of local ethnic minority organisations and support groups. To find your CRC look in your phone book, ask at your town hall or local library, or contact the above.

Disability Alliance Educational and Research Association
Universal House
88–94 Wentworth Street
London EI 7SA
(0171) 247 8763 (Advice line)
(0171) 247 8776
Information and advice on benefits for all people with disabilities. Publish the Disability Rights Handbook – an annual guide to rights, benefits, and services for those with disabilities and their families.*

Family Fund
PO Box 50
York YOI 2ZX
(01904) 621115
A government fund independently administered by the Joseph Rowntree Memorial Trust. Gives cash grants to families caring for severely handicapped children under 16. (See page 132.)

**Health Search Scotland
Information Officer
The Priory
Canaan Lane
Edinburgh EH10 4SG**
(0345) 708010
A national health information service which can provide details of the many groups and voluntary organisations that exist to support people with health problems.

**Maternity Alliance
15 Britannia Street
London WC1X 9JP**
(0171) 837 1265
Information on all aspects of maternity care and rights. Advice on benefits, maternity rights at work.*

**National Council for One Parent Families
255 Kentish Town Road
London NW5 2LX**
(0171) 267 1361
Free information for one parent families on financial, legal and housing problems.*

**One Plus
39 Hope Street
Glasgow G2 6AE**
(0141) 221 7150
Write or phone for free confidential advice on pregnancy, housing, benefits, taxation, maintenance, and other problems. Advice department closed Wednesdays.

Social Security: Freeline
For general advice on all social security benefits, pensions and national insurance including maternity benefits and Income Support, phone Freeline Social Security on 0800 666555 between 8.30am and 5pm on weekdays. Calls are free. There is an answerphone service out of hours.
Advice in Gujerati, Urdu or Punjabi:
Phone Freeline 0800 289188 between 9am and 4pm weekdays. For Punjabi only telephone Freeline 0800 521360 during the same hours.

Social security: local offices
For general advice on all social security benefits, pensions and national insurance, including maternity benefits and Income Support, telephone, write or call in to your local social security office. The address will be in the phone book under (social security). Hours are usually 9.30am to 3.30pm. In busy offices there may be a very long wait if you call in.

Social services
A social worker at your local social work department will give you information on topics including benefits, housing, financial difficulties, employment, relationship problems, childcare and useful organisations. Look up social work in the phone book under the name of your local regional council or ask at your local library. Phone, write or call in. There may also be a social worker based at the hospital whom you could talk to either during your antenatal care or when you or your baby are in hospital. Ask your midwife or other hospital staff to put you in contact.

SAFETY AND FIRST AID

**Scottish Red Cross Society
Alexandra House
204 Bath Street
Glasgow G2 4HL**
(0141) 332 9591
Among other activities, runs first aid courses through local branches. *

**Child Accident Prevention Trust
CAPT
18–20 Farringdon Lane
London EC1R 3AU**
(0171) 608 3828
Promotes child safety. Help and advice for parents.*

**Parents Anonymous
8 Manor Gardens
London N7 6LA**
(0171) 263 8918
A 24-hour telephone answering service for parents who feel they can't cope or who feel they might abuse their children.

**The Royal Society for the Prevention of Accidents (RoSPA)
Slateford House
53 Lanark Road
Edinburgh EH14 1TL**
(0131) 455 7457
Advice on the prevention of accidents of all kinds. Runs the Tufty Club for under-five year olds.*

**St Andrew's Ambulance Association
St Andrew's House
Milton Street
Glasgow G4 0HR**
(0141) 332 4031
Runs local first aid courses. Look for your nearest branch in the phone book, or contact the above address.*

SMOKING

**ASH
8 Frederick Street
Edinburgh EH2 2HB**
(0131) 225 4725
Assists smokers wishing to stop and promotes non-smoking as the norm in society. Information and resource centre for the public.*

**QUIT
102 Gloucester Place
London W1H 3DA**
(0171) 487 3000
Smoker's quitline
Advice on stopping smoking and details of local stop smoking support services. Phone between 9.30am and 5.30pm on weekdays. Recorded advice available at other times. Or write for information.

**Smokeline
Network Scotland
Ruthven Lane
Glasgow G12 9JQ**
0800 848484
**Freephone
(12pm–12am daily)**
Provides support and encouragement to those who wish to stop smoking or who have recently stopped and want to stay stopped. Callers can receive a free 'You can stop smoking' booklet.*

SUPPORT AND INFORMATION

**Caesarean Support Network
c/o Sheila Tunstall
2 Hurst Park Drive
Huyton
Liverpool L36 1TF**
(0151) 480 1184
Emotional support and practical advice to mothers who have had a caesarean delivery. Network of local contacts.*

**Equal Opportunities Commission
Overseas House
Quay Street
Manchester M3 3HN**
(0161) 833 9244
Information and advice on issues of discrimination and equal opportunities.*

**Family Welfare Association
501–505 Kingsland Road
London E8 4AU**
(0171) 254 6251
National charity providing free social work services, e.g. counselling for relationship difficulties and advice on benefits, housing and other problems. Provides grants for people in need throughout the UK.*

**Home-Start UK
Consultant for Scotland
84 Drymen Road
Glasgow G61 2RH**
(0141) 942 3450
A voluntary home-visiting scheme. Volunteers visit families with children under five and offer friendship, practical help, and emotional support. Write for list of local schemes.

**Institute for Complementary Medicine
PO Box 194
London SE16 1QZ**
(0171) 237 5165
Charity providing information on complementary medicine and referrals to qualified practitioners or helpful organisations.*

**National Childbirth Trust (NCT)
Regional Coordinator
Ascol
Pulpit Hill
Oban**
(01631) 62003
Help, support, and advice for mothers, including breastfeeding information and support, antenatal classes, postnatal groups. Write for details of your nearest branch.*

**Patients' Association
18 Victoria Park Square
Bethnal Green
London E2 9PF**
(0181) 981 5676
Advice service for patients who have difficulties with their doctor. *

**Twins and Multiple Births Association (TAMBA)
Regional Representative
2 Glebe Grove
Edinburgh EH12 7SH**
(0131) 3343070
Advice and support for parents of multiples. Network of local Twins Clubs.*

**Women's Aid Federation
12 Torphichen Street
Edinburgh EH3 8JQ**
(0131) 221 0401
(between 10am and 1pm)
Information, support and refuge for abused women and their children.

**Women's Health
52 Featherstone Street
London EC1Y 8RT**
(0171) 251 6580 (call 11am–5pm, not open Tuesday)
Information and support on many aspects of women's health. Provides a network of individual women who support others with similar health problems.*